S.O.S.

SURVIVORS OF STORMS

Darin McAllister

S.O.S. Survivors of Storms

Copyright © 2017 by Darin McAllister

Unless otherwise noted, all Scripture quotations are from the King James Version of the Bible.

Some names and identifying details have been changed to protect the privacy of individuals. I have tried to recreate events, locals and conversations from my memories of them. In order to maintain their anonymity, in some instances, I have changed the names of individuals.

Cover Art by DeShon Gales for DG Creative Studio

Art Direction by Christopher Coleman for I Think for You Consulting, LLC

Editing and typesetting by Fresh Reign Publishing, www.freshreign.com
Proofing by Dr. Judith McAllister and Audrea Walker

ISBN 978-0-9796717-3-9

THIS BOOK IS DEDICATED TO

PHYLLIS

THE TRUE SURVIVOR

THANK YOU FOR ALL OF YOUR, PRAYERS, LOVE, AND SUPPORT!

Da

ACKNOWLEDGEMENTS

My heart is overwhelmed with gratitude when I think of all the very special people who have impacted my life, who modeled what true survivors look like. You came along and stood by my side and demonstrated the behavior in a real and tangible way.

First, I am thankful to God for His goodness and mercy which are new every morning. Great is His faithfulness to me!

To my incredible wife, Dr. Judith Christie McAllister, who demonstrates the love of Christ Jesus here on earth daily. Thank you for sticking with me every step of the way and being a partner in raising our blessings, three incredible and beautiful children who understand what it means to trust God.

Thank you, Michael, for growing up sooner than you had to.

Thank you, Christina, for your kindness in every circumstance.

Thank you, Destiny, for being an example of excellence in all that you do.

To Bishop Charles Blake, Sr., Lady Mae Blake, and the entire West Angeles Church family, thank you for embracing my entire family and welcoming us *Home*. Your kindness will never be forgotten and your love will always be celebrated.

To Bishop Joseph and Dr. Stephanie Walker, thank you for embracing my family and me in the storm. You demonstrated what true ministry is and how it is done.

To my brothers and sisters who never stopped believing in me, I am so grateful to have siblings like you! My sisters, Pam and Phyllis, who never let me spend a Thanksgiving alone and made the three-hour drive in six hours (smile). Thank you to my brothers, Irvin and Kevin, for encouraging your baby brother and reminding me that I could make it.

Special thanks to Earvin and Cookie Johnson. You took the time to speak words of encouragement and told me to finish writing what God had given.

Thank you to Pauletta and Denzel Washington for your commitment to checking on my family while I was gone. Thank you to Michael and Stasia Washington for sponsoring my legal fundraiser, and thank you to everyone who contributed your love and generosity. It will never be forgotten.

A special thanks to Karla Allen for sticking with me through the writing process. Your ability to hear my heart and help me transcribe it is truly a gift from God.

To Devin Stewart, thank you for lending your twenty-years of publishing experience, to guide me along the way; and a very special thank you to Antracia Morrings for reading and making sure the message was coming across clearly.

To my *friend that sticks closer than a brother,* James Williams, thank you for praying for me, pushing me, and giving me the will to survive.

And...a final word of thanks to you, the reader. It is because of you that I survived. I survived to tell a story that will encourage you to fight and overcome the temptation to quit. God has a purpose and a plan for you and your storm.

You will survive!

iv /

TABLE OF CONTENTS

FOREWARD

With over 60 years of ministry, I have observed countless individuals weather the storms of life. As a sailor who sets out to sail on a clear day only to be overtaken by an unpredictable violent storm, so I have witnessed the sudden storms of failing health, financial failure, drug addiction, and even death in the lives of unsuspecting people. However, through every storm, I have also had the profound privilege to witness the faithfulness of God to his children. Eventually, through the darkness, the light of victory appears.

I am reminded of the Apostle Paul, who was shipwrecked in a storm while he was a prisoner. This is the man who had an encounter with God and was called to preach the Gospel of Jesus Christ. Like many of us, he did not have an easy road to travel after his conversion; he was tempted, persecuted, and often wrestled with death. In this account, Paul was forced overboard in a storm, only to survive on "broken pieces." God spared Paul's life in the storm, so He could use him to bring healing and salvation to others. We are not always delivered from the storms, but like the Apostle Paul, we go through them with God's amazing grace.

While in the storms of life, we may experience the feelings of isolation, abandonment, and depression. Because oftentimes, during those obscure and lonely days, others may not understand and will pass judgements that are neither accurate or supportive. Without relying on the grace of God, one can become angry, bitter, and ultimately lose faith in God. S.O.S is a clear reminder, God will not abandon you in the storm. In contrast, He will deliver you, give meaning to your storm, and empower you to help others survive.

The testimony of the survivor is powerful to those who are still in the storm. In a storm, heavy waves, blowing winds, and torrent conditions, can blind you to the very thing that will assist you in your survival. Therefore, the testimony of the survivor always activates hope and demonstrates the intentionality by which you must trust God in the midst of your storm.

I have known Darin and his wife, Judith, for over 30 years; I have watched them grow and develop into great leaders in our faith. S.O.S. gives you an intimate and vivid picture into the numerous challenges they have personally faced together over the years. Darin's transparency allows the reader to appreciate their living example to trust God in the face of betrayal, disappointment and loss. I believe S.O.S will bring healing to you as the reader and activate your faith to believe you can survive any storm, because God is faithful today just as he has always been.

I pray that your life is enriched and your heart encouraged as you read S.O.S. There is no doubt God has a purpose and plan for you. No matter what you have experienced in life or how bad you may feel things are, take courage, my friend. I do see you in the future, and you look much better than you look right now. May you be blessed as you read.

Bishop Charles E. Blake

Presiding Bishop and Chief Apostle, Church of God in Christ, Inc.

Pastor, West Angeles Church of God in Christ

Los Angeles, CA

x /

PREFACE

Hindsight, as they say, is 20/20; and when one is given the opportunity to reflect over the landscape of life, there arise certain poignant moments, giving purpose, meaning, and viability to the essence of who you are. One such moment occurred when I became acquainted with Darin McAllister as a student at Oral Roberts University.

Subsequently, through our 30 plus years together, we have endured many storms, both personally and collectively; but we have traversed through them all with a sense of faith and hope, that if God brought us to it, He would certainly bring us through it!

This book is not about a victim, but the attitude of a victor who weathered the storms of life and offers insight into how to survive when life presents the unexpected. Through the season of struggle and not fully being able to discern the plan of God, for the storm, I have witnessed Darin maintain the posture of the consummate optimist. He never gave up, even during those dark times of depression and despair, holding fast to Romans 8:28 – "And we know that all things work together for good to them that love God, to them who are the called according to His purpose."

Having had the honor of walking with Darin through much of his journey, I can attest to the faithfulness of God in our lives. I am so proud of Him and marvel at what I see emerging on the horizon, because he was authentic in every aspect of the storm.

You will be blessed as you read this literary gem. It is real, raw, thought-provoking and will encourage you to put your trust in God no matter what!

As I have prayed for Darin, I now pray for you, that the wind of the Spirit of God be consistently at your back, giving you the strength and the stamina needed to forge ahead...through the storm, into your victory!

Dr. Judith Christie-McAllister
President – Never Worship
Enterprises, LLC (N.E.W.)
President – International Music Department C.O.G.I.C.

INTRODUCTION

S.O.S is the distress signal used internationally by ships at sea that experience fierce, life-threatening circumstances or storms. The S.O.S Morse Code is transmitted as a last resort for help. It is a plea from violently tossed ships. When crew members exhaust all efforts, an S.O.S (*Save Our Ship*) an urgent appeal for help, is broadcast. It is a desperate call for others to risk their own safety and well-being to save others.

Like a distressed ship in a violent storm, people may experience those S.O.S seasons in life, while others have yet to become familiar with this type of episode. Although certain storms can be anticipated and managed, other storms may completely blind-side an individual. This type of storm provides little or no warning. It slams into a person like a freight train on the beach. It is the *worst day* of your life. These seasons require a S.O.S.

A S.O.S experience is not your typical awful day. In fact, time freezes, and at the same time never ends. The shock and disbelief cause pains inside of you that could be misdiagnosed as an upset stomach, constipation, or indigestion. But the diagnosis is incorrect. This feeling does not affect any internal organs; it affects your soul, the recesses of the heart. Those who have experienced authentic S.O.S seasons never forget. The events leading up to the storm and immediately afterwards are etched in your mind with meticulous detail—causing you to relive it with certain triggers such as smells, sounds, and sights.

The words *time heals all wounds* have some truth, but they do not apply to this day or time. Time does not necessarily bring healing, but it causes you to reflect on the simple fact, you survived. You can now be placed in the class of special select individuals called survivors.

The mentality and disposition of a survivor is not to be confused with that of a victim. Victims look for every opportunity to tell their story and receive attention and sympathy of others. Survivors are not looking for pity, but for the opportunity to inspire others. Survivors are transparent enough to show their scars. True survivors move past their scars, displaying themselves as victors not victims.

The personal experiences in this book are the real events of survivors, who courageously emerge from obscurity to a place of significance and purpose. As you read through the painful events, my prayer is that you will receive hope and courage to become a member of this elite S.O.S group, *SURVIVORS OF STORMS.*

A Mother's Plea

As a police officer on the streets of Los Angeles, California, in the early '90s, I had a chance to see it all. I did not read about it, I was not told about it, I did not have to wonder about it. I was literally given a front row seat to a wild ride every night that characterized the streets of L.A. I was initiated by the wildness of the Hollywood Division, where everyone on the street was a *star*. They came to Hollywood with big dreams and had fallen into the trappings of dreams turned nightmares. They had been used, abused, and put out on the streets like trash. I hate to admit it, but many reeked of trash, so officers found it easy to treat these people as though they were trash. There were few complaints about how they were treated by the police, because the police were still more kind than most of the people they would encounter as they walked the streets looking for their next fix.

I was told to get I.D.'s from a group of prostitutes that had caused a traffic accident. When one of the ladies of the night refused to give me her I.D., my training officer told me to search her. I requested a female officer to do the search. My training officer insisted that I search her because she could be dangerous and have weapons. I was hesitant because this was not necessarily procedure. The lady of the night was not very attractive. Layered with make-up to cover-up numerous flaws, she had quite a bit of clothing on for such a warm Southern California night. Even though she did not provide I.D., she readily complied with my search when I told her, "Turn around and put your hands on top of your head."

The smell of body odor and cheap perfume was nauseating. I had just finished checking the waistband, and asked, "Do you have any needles or anything sharp in your pockets?" Just as she answered no, I was doing a quick pat of the crotch area and immediately pushed *him* away in shock and disbelief. The screams of laughter came roaring from the other training officers who had come to see me broken into life on the streets of the Hollywood Division.

With a raspy bass voice, he said, "You didn't have to push me so hard. You act like you never felt one of those before." I was completely humiliated, disrespected, and ready to get even.

Before I could think of my retaliation, "Officer requesting back-up 415 fight Palladium night club."

I worked the melting pot of the Wilshire Division. This was the only division in the city that had residents from over 15 countries that spoke at least 10 different languages. The income ranged from some of the most expensive property in the United States to extreme poverty. In some cases, as many as 10 people could live in a one bedroom apartment. The West Los Angeles Division was primarily commercial and reflective of UCLA and wealth. Whenever you stopped someone, you usually heard, "Do you know who I am?" My favorite weekend spot was the beach in The Pacific Division. I got paid to go to the beach and walk the boardwalk. Tourists loved the LAPD and wanted to take pictures with us.

My primary hours were from 6:00 p.m. to 3:00 a.m. During these hours, I responded to more calls in one shift than my counterparts in other cities responded to in a week. When I arrived on the scene of a shooting, traffic accident, fire, or fight, I would immediately look for the survivors. It was not the obvious ones that were up and walking around that distinguished individuals as survivors. The survivors may have been bloodied or bruised. You did not hear complaints about blood on their good shoes, torn Versace dresses, or the beautiful coats that now smelled like smoke. You could see the look in their eye that said, "I am just glad to be alive."

One Friday night on Memorial Day weekend, we anticipated a hectic night due to the holiday. As we approached Adams and Crenshaw Boulevards, I heard three rapid shots that sounded like they could have come from my standard issued Berretta 92F. We were only three blocks from West Angeles Church of God in Christ where my family and I attended church at the time, so I had an obvious concern.

Our tires screeched and the engine roared as we whipped a U-turn in the middle of Adams Blvd., heading in the direction of the gun shots. One block East, we saw the desperation of a middle-aged man in a wife-beater tank top standing in the middle of the street. Before we could acknowledge the waving hands, we heard the crack of our police radio, "Shots fired Crenshaw and Adams." I calmly acknowledged we were on the scene.

As I exited the car, I heard the distinguishing sound that had become, unfortunately, common to me, a piercing mother's scream. A mother was in *travail*, and pleading for her son's life. As her son's limp body lay between the grass and the sidewalk, this was her *S.O.S* moment.

As I approached the wailing mother and the seemingly lifeless body of the young man, the mother's eyes caught mine and she pleaded, "Save him! We are losing him!" When I looked at the young man, I saw the blood pouring out of his head and ears. Even though the mother gave an *S.O.S* plea, I ignored her and resorted to my training. I routinely pulled out my radio and requested an estimated time of arrival (ETA) on the ambulance.

As to continue to avoid the mother's plea for help, I made myself busy by pushing back the crowd that had gathered, and marking off the area with yellow caution tape. The moment I was done, I realized what I had done. By tying the yellow tape around the scene, it was a sign of defeat to everyone present, but a sign of victory for Death. Again, the mother's eyes caught mine, but this time, I could not avoid her desperate gaze. She quietly cried, "Will you help him? I don't think he is breathing." She was basically asking me to give her son Cardiopulmonary Resuscitation (CPR). However, we are trained only to give CPR to fellow officers.

Although I had no children of my own at the time, the human and compassionate side of me was just about to give into this mother's plea, when I heard the siren of the ambulance. Relieved, I broke eye contact with this frantic pleading mother, and I busied myself by making an opening for the ambulance to get through the crowd. The paramedics came and went with no real sense of urgency. This shooting was, as far as they were concerned, routine.

As I walked away from the ambulance, I started talking to potential witnesses. However, as usual, I was met with selective memory characteristic of those dreading retaliation. Out of fear, no one wanted to talk or at least be seen talking to the police. As I took one last look at the ambulance slowly pulling off, the shadow of the mother in the front seat reminded me that I would be coming back to interview this mother. The young man was not dead, but in my mind and experience he was on his way.

At the scene, there was a puddle of blood showing what was left of his life on the streets of L.A. A neighbor came out with a bucket of water with bleach in it to wash down the sidewalk. My partner and I had to stop him because this was crime scene evidence. Understandably, he wanted to get rid of any reminders of his block being a deadly place to live.

A Mother's Victory

It was going to be a scorching summer in L.A. Every officer knew that a blistering summer meant the city would be full of unlawful activity. On this particular day, I was asked to pick up a report from the hospital for one of my academy classmates. They knew me at the hospital because we were there to interview someone daily. I was waiting for the receptionist to look up the file on the computer and I heard my street name, "Officer! Hey, officer!" Surprisingly, this was not the common distressed tone I was accustomed to hearing. In a less defensive posture, I turned and greeted a middle-aged African-American woman that was all smiles. She spoke to me as if she knew me. She did not look familiar; nor could I immediately place her. I resorted to doing a mental scan to determine where I had seen her, "Did I know her from church, the streets, school or was she just a well-wishing, friendly citizen?"

Before I could make the determination, she was hugging me. It wasn't an embrace that I was accustomed to in uniform and, in some ways, I was shocked by her actions. Then she said the words, "It's a miracle! He survived!" With a smile that electrified the room, she said, "I thought we had lost him, but the bullet actually ricocheted off his hard head." Only a mother can insult her own child after a life and death experience. The joy and laughter with which she spoke was infectious. At some point, I recognized she was the mother from the shooting three days earlier. I realized I was waiting to be summoned by the homicide detectives; however, I was never called. Her son was alive. The young man that laid on the street in a lifeless condition was alive.

The mother did not have the mindset of a victim, because she was a survivor. Her son cheated death and survived. The previously pleading mother was now celebrating the victory over death. Like a true survivor, she did not talk about how the shooting occurred, or why her son was on the street. On the contrary, she was celebrating that her son was alive. She wanted to share the joy of her son's survival with me. I joined her in the celebration for her son's life. It was a true testament that miracles do happen. Her last words to me were, "Thank you for caring. Thank you for helping my son and me. You were like an angel." I did not consider myself an angel, but I could not help celebrating that this young man had survived.

Reaction vs. Response

Survivors have a unique attraction. They attract others because they are ordinary people who respond, not react, with great poise in crisis. There is a clear difference between reacting as opposed to responding in the middle of a crisis. Reactions are made without thought or consideration of consequences. Reactions can be dangerous and may seem natural because they are based on the true nature and character of a person.

Reactions are demonstrated when we are in the doctor's office and our reflexes are tested. The doctor may ask us to relax, and then he taps us with a rubber mallet just below the knee cap. Instantaneously, our leg snaps forward without any thought or direction from us. This is a reaction not a response.

On one of my routine patrols, on what appeared to be a quiet residential street, the front door of one of the peach colored stucco homes opened as if the house had exploded. An African American man in his mid-40's in his blue delivery uniform was chasing what appeared to be a 20-year old African American man who had the cringes of fear and pain painted on his face with every stride he took. The older man was yelling the words, "I'm going to kill you." The young man ran to our car for help. We brought no immediate refuge for this young man, so the older man jumped on him like a lion on his prey.

The older man had no regard for our presence, so I intervened and pulled the older man off the young man and handcuffed him. He spouted endless profanities of what he was going to do to the younger man. I made every effort to calm him and get to the bottom of why he was so upset with this young man. After 15 minutes, I started getting tearful bits and pieces of information from him. The reality of this man's reaction was starting to make sense. His 17-year-old daughter was pregnant by this young man. A father did what was in his protective nature to do. He reacted to an offense that had taken place against his daughter. There was no consideration of consequences just a reaction.

A survivor does not react solely on his or her nature. In contrast, a survivor responds because a new perspective enables the survivor to resist the common tendencies of their nature. Perspective is simply the way you view something or someone. Your sight and insight are determining factors of your vision. If your perspective is limited, your vision will be limited. One is always influenced by the other.

However, with a new perspective, one can learn how to respond properly without being hauled into a careless reaction. A proper response is one that pauses to give thought before taking any action. Thought that takes into consideration the consequences and the outcome.

The Honeymooners

Numerous life principles are learned through storms and many of these principles came very early in my adult life — shortly after my college sweetheart and I were married. We were living as true honeymooners with the one-bedroom apartment over the bus stop on busy Olympic Boulevard in Los Angeles. We knew the bus schedule by heart and used it as a makeshift alarm in the morning. We could set a watch by the time it made its first pick-up and its last run for the night. We could look out our small living room window and see the pace it kept with unpredictable LA traffic.

We did not have a care in the world, until the third month of our marriage when Judy started having excruciating pain in her abdomen. The hospital was less than three blocks from our apartment and I rushed her to Emergency. I held her hand and all kind of thoughts went through my mind, all of which made me feel ill-equipped to properly comfort her. In my attempt to appease her pain, I tried to make her laugh. I found out the hard way you do not make a woman having abdominal pain laugh. My attempt to appease her, further tortured my wife, Judy.

After running some tests, the doctor came back and sat down to talk with us as if we had been long time friends. His first words were, "I have good news and bad news." The good news is, you are pregnant. The bad news is you have a tumor growing with the baby that is also increasing in size. My young mind was still trying to process what all that meant, "Was Judy's life in danger? Was the baby's life in danger? Were they both in danger? What was I supposed to do next, and how much time did I have to decide?" All my questions were answered before I could even ask them.

"The tumor and the baby can't grow together. The tumor should be removed. But, if we remove the tumor there is a good possibility you will miscarry."

Wow! Decisions had to be made, and they had to be made quickly.

Without hesitation, the Dr. stated, "I want to operate in the next hour." Judy looked to me for answers. We were in the storm. Unfortunately, we were too far out to turn around. Furthermore, we were not sure if we could make it to the other side.

Often, storms will leave you with few options and even less time to make decisions. I looked at Judy and as calmly and comforting as I could, I asked, "What do you want to do?"

"It hurts really bad," she responded. I could not bear to see Judy in so much pain, so I asked the doctor what he thought the chances were for the baby if Judy had the surgery. There was a 50/50 chance that the baby would survive, but he would do everything he could. The rest would be up to Judy.

The ball was thrown back into our court, seemingly, without a moment's hesitation. I decided to do what any good son would do. I called home to talk to my mother. Her words were simple, "Do what you think is best, and I will pray." I felt like Peter. I was out of the boat trying to walk on water. I was out of the boat looking at Jesus, and this wave was crashing over my head three months into my marriage. I went back to the teaching of the great late Oral Roberts. While attending Oral Robert's University, I learned God uses prayer and medicine, at times, to heal. This would be the path I would choose to take. With that, we made one more call to Judy's mom to strengthen our prayer support.

I went with Judy to the cold sterile prep room making every effort to comfort her as best I could. Before I knew it, the nurse gave me the signal that it was time for me to go. I spoke my silent prayer to God, kissed her gently, then left the room believing for a miracle. The drugs for the surgery were starting to take effect. Her eyes were now glassy and her speech slightly slurred. I was thankful that she was no longer in pain.

As I walked to the family waiting room to sit alone, I was greeted by the only family that could be present on such short notice. Bishop and Mrs. Blake walked in as two concerned parents, "How's Judy?" Bishop Blake asked. I wanted to fall into their arms and weep. Up to this point, I had been tasked with making life, and what I consider death, decisions. I was emotionally and physically exhausted. I just needed someone to tell me that at 23 years of age, I had done the right thing and was doing everything a new husband should do for his wife.

The doctor came out two hours later and said all went well. He made it clear that we made the right decision because the tumor was much larger than he had thought. In a solemn tone, he said, "These next three days will be critical for the baby." Upon hearing those words, I was happy with the decision that we made, but I now had knots in my stomach about how the next three days would go. I asked to see Judy.

As I walked into the recovery room, Judy was wrapped tightly in warm blankets. I was able to get a slight smile out of her that signaled all was well. Her first words were, "Is the baby ok?" I assured her the baby was fine, and she was going to be fine, as well. Everything was well. He did it again. Prayer never fails and causes everything to work out exactly like we expected it would. I went to get something to eat and something nice for Judy to wear while she was in the hospital. Everything was going just fine and I was going to be a daddy. I thought about it with overwhelming excitement and mind-numbing fear all at the same time.

I had my gift nicely wrapped and tried to extinguish all signs of the well-seasoned meal I had just consumed at the diner, which was about a two-block walk from the hospital. The air was balmy for late September and seemed to have a calming effect on me. When I arrived at the hospital, I could see they had put Judy on the maternity floor and I heard the crying newborn babies.

Wow! That would be us soon, getting ready to take our bundle of joy home. Ready or not, a little one was on the way.

Judy's door was closed and the room was dark when I peaked in, except for the light created by the Olympic Blvd street lamps. Through the stillness, I heard what sounded like a soft whimper. As I approached Judy's bed, I could see the glistening of tears on her cheeks. "I don't think the baby is going to make it, my stomach is cramping really bad and the nurse...." Before she could finish her sentence, Judy gasped for air. Pain shot through her body as if someone had hit her in the stomach with a baseball bat. A nurse walked in as if she was half drill sergeant and half undertaker.

Free of any emotion, she said, "She's going to pass the baby. Let me know if you need anything and we'll get you cleaned up."

It was a somber moment without a happy ending. We were still newlyweds, but our honeymoon had come to a crashing halt. I sat there on the bed holding Judy's hand as she wept. We had lost our first child. Understandably, I had no words, no understanding, no fix, remedy, solution, or answers for what just happened. We were feeling the pain of a common storm many parents have endured. The loss of a child.

Some may minimize the loss and discount the bond and connection that is made between a mother and a fetal child. There is a bond and a sense of loss that causes grieving to take place. I was at a loss because there was no training class or experience to prepare me to deal with this loss. There was no one to call to get guidance, comfort or instruction. The few that we could share something so personal with were not adequately prepared to give words of comfort. It was a long road to travel that would be filled with painful potholes of disappointment.

Disappointments

The first time the word "disappointment" came into full affect for me was at the young age of 8 years old. The words were spoken by my mother. She tearfully expressed her disappointment as I walked in the door with a hole in the knee of my brand-new school pants. The first time I wore them, I put them through a grueling test. They were supposed to be tough skins. My intentions were to see just how tough they were. The real test would come for me later. My *skin* was going to be tested by my mama.

Her disappointment was so deep that she did not whip me. She expressed her disappointment with words so strong, I wanted to yell, "Just beat me!" She talked about the great sacrifice she made to get the pants for me. She went back to her childhood and painted a vivid picture of how only the rich and privileged could get a new pair of pants. Most clothes were handed down from sibling to sibling. Even though I was a young boy, it crushed me to know I was the object of her disappointment.

True disappointment comes from a place in the heart that causes others to identify with the pain, frustration, and anguish that was experienced. You truly feel their pain and hurt. It drives you to a place of wanting to make it right. I was expected to recognize how fortunate I was to have such a nice brand new pair of pants. I was expected to value the sacrifices that had been made for me to wear those pants. Unfortunately, I had no appreciation for just how privileged I was.

We all have experienced disappointments, and it usually is a result of our expectations not being met. We expected one result, but were handed a different outcome. Life experiences reveal that not every story has a happy ending. But, the true test is how to keep moving forward when you experience one disappointment after another.

Losing a baby was not the only disappointment Judy and I experienced. It was one of four. We were at the point of complete despair and had all but given up on having children. Even in the place of complete despondency, we made a choice that went against the grain. Despite the pain, heartache, and frustration, we refused to throw in the towel and quit. Disappointment would not guide our decision to hope again.

When you are not in the middle of the storm, finding hope is much easier said than done. It is often as you rely on the core beliefs that are embedded within, hope is activated. When you talk to survivors, oftentimes, they will tell you they went to their internal drive to retrieve their fundamental beliefs, to help them find the hope that would help them survive the storm.

Beliefs

As I have gone through life, I noticed there are parallels between my training as a minister of the Gospel of Jesus Christ, and as a police officer. The study of theology at Oral Roberts University (ORU) and the police training I received from the Los Angeles Police Academy share a fundamental principle: your training and preparation will reveal what you believe when challenged. My training and study further reinforced foundational principles I learned at home known as *home training*. My home training was not formal with consistent dates and deadlines for tests like the university and the Police Academy. However, it was modeled and observed throughout key times in my life by trusted sources such as my mother, my father, my brothers, and my sisters.

Over the years, I have learned that when you are challenged, you will revert to how you were trained to respond to situations. For example, when you watch athletes train and practice, they often respond in games based on how they have practiced.

At the age of 18, I was told repeatedly, "Something good is going to happen to you." I also remember hearing, "Make no little plans here." These words were coupled with biblical principles from Matthew 21:22, You can pray for anything; and if you have faith, you will receive it. As a result, I believed I was supposed to have huge faith and believed my only limitation was my imagination. Consequently, I demonstrated my belief through my actions in the second semester of my sophomore year of college.

Even though I had a full scholarship with a stipend to attend Morehouse College in Atlanta, Georgia, I chose to attend Oral Roberts University (ORU) with only a $500.00 music scholarship. I attended ORU because I believed ORU was the school I was destined to attend. Even so, my faith was tested in my sophomore year at ORU. Tuition was due, but I had no way of paying the bill. I knew the fate of others who faced similar crises, but never returned to school.

At the same time, my aunt, who was not the kindest woman in my childhood, asked me how college was going. I respectfully told her, "Okay." My response was obviously not sufficient as she pressed me for more information. She asked what I was studying, and when I was leaving to return to school. In order to stop what felt like a police interrogation, I answered, "I'm not sure. They will not allow me back in until I pay my tuition in full." My aunt frowned as if she had been poked with a cattle prod.

With pure disgust, she asked, "How much do you have to pay?" I explained that I owed $500.00. In a shocking moment for me, she reached into her personal safe and pulled out a wad of $100.00 bills. In a gruff voice, she said, "Come here." I watched and stood paralyzed as she counted out five hot, sweaty $100 bills into my hand. I did not know whether to say thank you or drop the money on the floor in gross repugnance. However, before I could even respond, in her stern voice she said, "Now get on back to that school and get some good grades."

In reality, I should not have been in shock. With all my heart, I believed ORU was a part of my destiny. I believed I would be back after the break, and I believed that I would come up with the money I needed. I had been trained to believe. I just had no idea how it was going to happen. My training at ORU strengthened the foundation of my belief system. Even though I could not explain how what I was believing for would take place, I knew it would happen. In the same way, you may not know how you are going to get through your storm, but the most important thing is to believe that you will. This is the demonstration of the faith principle in action, which is simply believing despite contrary circumstances, conditions and responses.

This principle transformed my life in regards to how to survive storms. Learning this lesson early in life has allowed me to experience some amazing miracles. For example, I have experienced miracles of great employment and opportunities when others said I was not qualified or a good fit. The miracle of meeting amazing people like Earvin "Magic" Johnson, Jr., who overcame one of life's greatest health storms still amazes me. I was also privileged to meet Clifford Wilson who quietly pastors a church where some have never been. Even so, his impact has affected thousands through the ministry of discipleship. I have also experienced the miracle of traveling to foreign lands only to recognize that for some who live in subhuman conditions, the storm is never ending. The fight to survive is part of the daily drill. Experiencing these miracles equipped me with the ability to have a faith that goes beyond my own understanding. Ultimately, if you do not believe you will survive, you will not put forth the effort to overcome the opposition and challenges you face.

"Survival is dependent upon what you have been trained to do during a crisis." These are the words I heard in the first three days at the Los Angeles Police Academy. Those simple words, made me take my training seriously. When drill sergeants walked up to me and were so close that I could smell the woodsy cheap after shave they were wearing, I could not help but give them my undivided attention. Although, while in the Academy the penalty for not paying attention was severe and immediate, my superiors made it clear it was nothing compared to the penalties I would experience on the streets for any lack of attentiveness. Penalties that would immediately result in my own fatality, or possibly the fatality of others.

Within the first two weeks of being out of the academy, the validity of my training was immediately tested. One of the first areas I was assigned to worked was known as Grand Theft Auto Alley (GTA). In this area, cars were taken at will. Working the area was like a human cat and mouse game. Furthermore, we knew the stolen cars would most likely be used in a more serious crime.

One shift, I noticed a car and the driver who seemed like an odd fit. My suspicions were confirmed when I saw the right passenger side window was broken. The break in the window was a five-inch hole just above the door lock, causing the rest of the glass to spider. There was no additional damage to that area of the black Honda and as they said in the academy, "That's a clue."

Consequently, my partner and I started following and requested back-up before initiating a traffic stop. Even though I had not finished the radio transmission, my partner, who was driving, yelled, "Buckle up! We are going for a ride!" As the officer in the passenger seat, I was trained to be the navigator and to broadcast our location at all times. However, my mind went blank when I realized I had missed the first turn. I had no idea where we were. We were picking up speed and approaching about 50 mph. My partner turned on the lights and siren. Fortunately, I remembered to roll up the windows, so the dispatcher could hear my transmission over the siren.

On the first left turn, the speed pushed me into the door with an amount of force that I had never experienced. Everything seemed to move at mach speed. Just then, the dispatcher asked for an update on our location. Fortunately, the air unit heard that we were in pursuit and announced they were en route. Unfortunately, in my attempt to hold on, I dropped the mic.

Sadly, this drew looks of frustration from my veteran partner because he was working with a rookie.

Thoughts raced through my head, "It looked a lot more fun on television." At that moment, I found myself resorting to my training. I picked up the mic, gave a description of the car and the license plate, and broadcasted our location.

Amid the chaos, my partner yelled, "He's gonna bail out here soon." We were going much too fast for anyone to bail out of a car. The engine continued to roar like we were at the speedway, and the screeching tires cried on every turn. Even though I was seated in the car with the widows rolled up and the air conditioner on full blast, beads of sweat were popping out on my forehead like bullets. At that moment, I also noticed other squad cars joining in the pursuit. It was like a singing chorus of sirens. Some squad cars sang the high notes, while others sang the low notes, to create a melody that is every car thief's worst nightmare. Although in the first 30 seconds it seemed like that car thief was going to escape, the preparation during training, the additional squad cars, along with the helicopter support, changed the initial outcome.

Just when I thought I could take a breath, the driver of the stolen car rolled out of the moving car. With catlike agility, the suspect began running, jumping over bushes, through front yards, and along the side to the back of neighborhood houses. The car the thief was driving continued down the hill, playing bumper cars as it took on a mind of its own. Unfortunately, the thief's car side-swiped parked cars as it rolled out of control. It did not discriminate by skipping the trash cans that were at the curb waiting for pick-up. Instead, it hit the garbage cans like a bowling ball going for the strike. At that moment, I asked myself, "What are we supposed to do now?" Our police car suddenly came to a screeching halt, at which time, the smell of rubber and burning metal from our squad car's brakes filled the air.

It seemed like my partner morphed his way out of the car. On the other hand, I had not even taken off my seat belt. The next thing I knew, I was looking at the heels of his boots as he went over a fence. My partner was instinctively responding based on his experience, while I was thinking through my training. I was trained never to separate from my partner, so I had to get out and catch up. The siren was still blaring as I jumped the fence.

The suspect was about 50 yards in front of me and my partner was about 25 yards ahead of me. Before I knew it, they both turned a corner and were out of sight. At that moment, I remembered I was still the broadcaster and was supposed to give our location. Again, I was in trouble. I had no idea where we were. Thankfully, I was bailed out by the observer from the helicopter, who broadcast our location. Instinctively, I turned the right way. My partner had his gun drawn and was giving the command for the suspect to get on the ground. The suspect extended his hands in the air without hesitation and fell on the ground like he was ready to take a nap. His chest and mid-section were rising and falling rapidly. I was cautiously watching him before I approached to handcuff him. I approached and yelled, "Don't move," over the helicopter hovering above. His legs and arms were extended like superman and his sagging shorts had completely exposed his boxers. Although he moved fast for a big guy, it was clear he simply ran out of gas.

During my body search for weapons, I found two rocks of cocaine and $1,500.00 in cash in his right front pocket. Shortly after, we arrived back at the stolen vehicle, an officer at the scene was holding a black 9mm handgun found in the suspect's car. I had survived my first pursuit and arrested my first suspect.

It took me a while to gather myself and come down from the adrenaline rush. I heard other officers describe their first pursuit as a rollercoaster ride. It was true. Even so, I could not wait to ride again. After this first experience, I recognized when things happen, they happen fast and unexpectedly. Oddly enough, I never imagined I would have the same experience countless times over the next six years. Fortunately, my training and preparation helped me successfully maneuver through each experience. As time went on, those who failed to implement the necessary tools learned in training were less successful. Ultimately, I believe the primary reason why people abandon training is stress. The stress of the moment often causes one to revert to previous habits, as opposed to applying what is learned in training.

This was never more apparent than in the LA riots of 1992. It was a day that most Americans, especially Los Angeles police officers, will never forget. Rodney King's beating hit the national news like a tidal wave. As I watched my fellow police officers repeatedly beat Rodney King, I was overwhelmed with emotions. What I witnessed was not a part of my training. As a result, there was now a tension in the air that was so thick you could slice it with a knife and serve it up. While some of the white officers were trying to figure out why it was such a *big deal,* the black officers were ashamed and filled with rage. As I watched Rodney King receive blow after blow, it caused my jaw to clinch tighter and tighter. I thought I was going to bite through my teeth. A storm was on the rise that made me evaluate, not only what I had been trained to do as a police officer, but how I had been trained to treat another human being. This storm was one of epic proportions that impacted, not just a city, but a nation.

As I reflected on how my parents trained me as a child, it made me realize that *home training* begins at an early age. While it may not always be conveyed verbally, the display of simple acts of saying good morning as a greeting to those you live with, and respecting those older with actions and words, are critical in learning how to treat others. I experienced this with my own father. He modeled for me how to treat people with dignity, fairness, and respect. Little did I know it would establish within me a set of priceless gems, words to live by in the form of strong core values. Therefore, I did not have to wait for a commentator or an activist on television to tell me that the police officers had violated Rodney King's civil rights. My inward core values established from a child set off an immediate alarm.

How you are raised as a child, educated, and trained as an adult all contribute to your ability to survive a storm. It makes no difference if you are being educated in a university, police academy, or in your own home. You will learn survival techniques to get you through storms you never imagined you could survive. The principles that may seem abstract and irrelevant at the time of training prove their value in the time of the storm. You will revert to what has been tried and proven. While others are going through trial and error, you will know what to do.

Knowing and Doing the Right Thing

We have often heard the phrase: *It's not what you know, but who you know.* The twin sister of this statement is: *It's not what you know, but what you do with what you know.* The things we have come to know are proven through our experience and observation. We know these things for the most part to be factual and true. The amazing thing is we sometimes act as if that which is true does not apply to us. We act as if we have some exemption from the laws and principles we know to be true.

Personally, I have watched individuals work themselves literally to death. They knew they should eat right, rest, and exercise. Although they are surrounded by books and magazines on health, they still suffer from a medical condition which could have been avoided if they would have done what they knew to do. You would think with the access to knowledge regarding healthy living, they would have avoided the storm of sickness and disease. The reality is we only apply about 20 percent of the knowledge we have. In other words, just because we have knowledge, does not mean we will apply what we know. How do we overcome this dilemma and avoid the storms? We must practice what we preach.

Most of us were raised in homes where we saw double standards. Consequently, as adults we have recreated these same homes. We would not approve of our children doing some of the same things we practice on a consistent basis. Instead of establishing a new standard, we throw down the trump card, "Do as I say. Not as I do." The saying may allow us to avoid the confrontation of children and subordinates, but it may not give us the ability to survive a storm. Unfortunately, when we do not practice what we preach, we compromise. We can come up with a lot of excuses, rationalizations, justifications, and reason our way through confrontations. However, in the end, we have done nothing more than compromise our beliefs by not practicing them. Real survivors will not compromise, but they will confront their storms head on.

How do you confront your storms? The first step to confronting your storm is by acknowledging you are in one. As a child, I had matured to the point of being able to recognize when dark clouds were gathering. These were signs for me to prepare for the storm that was coming. When I ignored these signs, I would get caught in the rain every time. I had no one to blame but myself. When I reflect deeply, I recognize I did not respond to the signs because I was pre-occupied with my own agenda. Nothing was more important than what I was doing at that moment. I never considered I would be sick and not able to play outside the next day. I was just living in the moment. I knew the consequences, but failed to act on them. Over time, I have come to realize, every storm has consequences, some of the consequences are manageable and others cannot be managed, tamed, or controlled. When the consequences become overwhelming, the thoughts come to mind, "I knew better. I could have avoided this if I would have just..."

A vital element that helps us, as individuals, overcome a storm is when we have someone or something in our life to hold us accountable for what we know. For example, when I did not use good judgment regarding the rainstorm that was imminent, others held me accountable. The accountability was not necessarily verbalized directly, but their actions spoke louder than words. My playmates started leaving me to play by myself when their mothers would call them to come inside. Before they left, they would tell me, "Look! It's getting ready to rain." My mom constantly told me to make sure I came in before it rained.

Often, we find ourselves resistant to being accountable to others. This develops at an early age. As a species that was created to have dominion, we do not always respond well to orders. As well, we may not value the source, or we may be too familiar with the source to listen. However, what is communicated is frequently true and beneficial.

As a parent, I noticed how this principle works first hand. I often make suggestions to my children, and they respectfully ignore me — because in my children's minds, I do not know what I am talking about. Although my advice is based on my wisdom and experience, I am still ignored. Like in the case with my son. The day of reckoning came when my son shared the great revelation of one of his basketball coaches regarding his free-throws. While my son shared his new-found insight, I found my face getting warm. The words he shared with me were familiar because I had told him the exact same thing for about two years. Now it was the truth because someone else was telling him. My frustration quickly faded because I realized I was that person, many times, whose own opinion was valued over parents, pastors, and family members.

The challenge comes in as a parent, friend, or just general observer when we see storms coming and we give the warning to no avail. I have listened to pastors and teachers give the warning cry, and they are ignored as if they are speaking another language. I experienced this as a father one morning when my son was jumping on the bed.

My son was about three years old. Every three-year-old, and even some thirty-year-olds, love to jump on the bed. However, as any good father, who has been left to care for his child, I knew my responsibilities were to feed my son and make sure he was safe while in my care. I thought, "No problem, I can manage with ease." However, I had, obviously, underestimated the unpredictability of my three-year-old son.

It was early one Sunday morning when I had the sole responsibility of taking care of my son. Like a good father, I fixed breakfast for my son, dressed him for church, and brought him to my bedroom to watch TV while I finished getting dressed. He sat down on the bed and watched TV like an angel. I was in the bathroom for about thirty seconds and returned to my bedroom to find him high flying on my bed. He was getting up in the air, having a ball. I kindly told him, "Hey man, don't jump on the bed. You have on your church clothes." He acknowledged me and sat down. I left the room again only to return to see a young acrobat in the making, flying high like he was a part of a circus act. Again, I told him, "Stop jumping on the bed. You're going to hurt yourself."

"Okay, Daddy," he said, in his sweet three-year-old voice.

As I returned to the bathroom to tie my tie, I suddenly heard a piercing scream. I raced to my bedroom to find blood pouring out of my son's mouth and him crying uncontrollably. Without hesitation, I swept him up in my arms, and took him to the bathroom to stop the bleeding and comfort him. Unfortunately, he had a one inch cut on his lip. During one of his jumps, he fell and bit his lip. Despite my warnings, I knew it was not the time to scold him as he was visibly shaken, and was, obviously, in need of a stitch or two. Now I had to figure out how I was going to tell his mother. A storm was brewing.

As a police officer, I had informed many parents that their children were found, arrested, hurt, and even deceased. But now I had to tell my own wife that our son was hurt while in my care. I steadied myself to speak calmly and brace myself for her response and rapid fire questions. I called my wife and told her what happened, and that I was going to take him to the hospital. The calm in her voice was shocking and she offered to come home. I responded that she did not need to, and I would take him to the emergency room. She told me to keep her up to date on how he was doing. I carried my son to the car and packed him like precious cargo. We arrived at Cedars Sinai's emergency room that had just finished with the wildness of Saturday night in L.A. I knew the schedules and the rotations from being on patrol in the area. The staff was fresh and ready to take walk-in patients.

By this time, my son's lip was swollen and clearly disfigured. It was typical for medical personnel to engage children who can talk to make sure there is no abuse. They asked my son, "What happened little guy?"

"I was jumping on the bed," he responded in his *sweet* voice. His response prompted no additional questions.

Because of the change of shift and it being a Sunday morning, the wait was not long. We were in the exam room within 15 minutes and a nurse was prepping my son for an experience he would never forget. In one of the kindest, sweetest voices I have ever heard, she asked, "Have you ever played the mummy game?"

He smiled and said, "no."

"Mummy game? That's a new one," I thought to myself. I personally had not played or even heard of the game. I quickly discovered the method to her madness as she had my son place his arms at his side and stand up straight and tall. She began wrapping white sheets around him from his shoulders to his ankles. I just shook my head and acknowledged that she was good. She then wrapped white medical tape around the sheets. Then she asked the question, "Can you get out?" My son pulled, tugged, twisted, and squirmed. With his best efforts, he could not break free. He was smiling and giggling with no clue of what was to come. She looked at me with a wink as she escorted him over to the exam table. Then, without hesitation she scooped him up on the exam table as the doctor walked in and greeted him with a, "Hi buddy." A bright light was turned on and shone in my son's face with the blinding power of high beams on a deer in the middle of the road.

Just like that, my son was totally disoriented, but was NOT numb to the needle that was placed directly into his laceration. He let out a scream that echoed throughout the emergency room hallways, "Daddy! Daddy! Help! Help! Make them stop! Help!" My heart sunk because I knew there was nothing I could do to relieve my son's pain. Feeling helpless, I turned my head to avoid seeing my son's face. Because of the deep love I have for my son, it was as if I felt what he felt physically and emotionally. Because I did not respond to his cries for help, I could see the sense of abandonment in his eyes as I looked back in his direction. With every stitch, he called my name, "Daddy!"

Finally, what seemed like hours was over in less than three minutes. The nurse who had wrapped him up told him they were finished and turned off the light. By this time, my son wanted no parts of her. She had tricked him and coerced him into a game that had terrible consequences. Even so, before the nurse left, he allowed her to place a small band aid on his protruding lip. As I walked over to pick him up and hold him, he laid his head on my shoulder and whispered, "They hurt me." My heart just ached because I now had to explain to a three-year-old that the doctor and nurse were helping him. Unfortunately, it would never make sense to him.

At some point, we have all experienced *jumping on the bed* without considering any of the consequences. Despite various warnings to stop, we continue to jump. Unfortunately, our bouncing one too many times, resulted in unfortunate consequences. Our fall from *jumping on the bed* may have been an addiction to a substance, a bad relationship, or financial devastation. The next thing we know, we are bloodied, wounded physically, and emotionally crying for help. That is when we are picked up by our Heavenly Father and comforted. But, we will still have to go through the process of healing and restoration.

I could have skipped taking my son to the doctor and putting him through additional trauma, but I would have put him at great risk. By taking him to the doctor, I prevented him from getting an infection and experiencing further complications. I also minimized the scar that would have formed if my son's lip had not been stitched properly. Ignoring consequences can cause self-inflicted storms that leave us feeling abandoned like my son. But, hopefully, we learn lessons that cause us to pay attention to the advice of those who desire to help us.

When You Have Nothing to Say, Listen

Death is a storm that gives finality to those who die, but is only the beginning of the storm for those who are living. During one of my classes at Oral Roberts University, I found the subject of death to be one where a script of words is terribly inadequate to console and comfort the sense of loss when one enters this storm.

His hair was snow white and his smile infectious. It made no difference if it was cold or hot outside, his red high cheeks always had a subtle red glow. At first glance, you would think you were looking at the man on the Quaker Oats box in a shirt and tie. Dr. Carpenter had a certain rhythm to his mature voice. He taught my practical ministries class that gave guidance on how to counsel in time of crisis. The class also taught us how to prepare for the special religious days such as baptism, christening, communion, weddings, and funerals. I enjoyed his class because it was not theory. We put together mini-sermons on these topics and presented them in class. I was doing well and achieving high marks until it came to the scenario of conducting a funeral service of a young man that died in a traffic accident. He and his family were new to the church. I was given brief facts about the family and the events leading up to the young man's death. My assignment was to prepare a eulogy appropriate for this young man and minister to the family, who were in a storm.

The ten days I was given to prepare seemed to disappear. On day eight, I asked Dr. Carpenter if I could meet with him after class. He readily agreed, and the next thing I knew, there we were in his tiny office, where the smell of stale coffee filled the air, and papers and notes were neatly stacked. With a smile that melted all my anxiety, he asked, "What can I do for you, young man?"

I explained my dilemma, "I have no idea what to do or say to these folks, Dr. Carpenter. I'm not good at talking to people about death." He nodded his head with a sense of complete understanding.

"Well, it sounds like you have taken this task seriously. Quite frankly, you are the only one that has come in to discuss their scenario." He continued by explaining, "If you think you can prepare and have all the right words to say, you will fail miserably every time." He further shared, "Death is real." As we sat there, he proceeded to tell me his personal story about his first encounter with the death of one of his congregants. "I was confronted with the death of a member the second month of becoming the pastor of an all-black church in St. Louis. I didn't say much of anything to the family for the first two weeks, but I was there. The eulogy was brief in a very emotional service. It wasn't my time to be the man with all the answers having it all figured out. I just had to be there to listen and comfort as best I could. My job was simply getting them from one day to the next."

In hindsight, I was never given the opportunity to ask any direct questions about the assignment. However, Dr. Carpenter's wise counsel and guidance prepared me for an experience I would see much more than I ever imagined. In life, it is certain that death, followed by the grieving process, is an event everyone will experience at some point. Unfortunately, most times one is not prepared.

Upon arriving at West Angeles Church of God in Christ in the late '80s as the personal assistant to senior Pastor, Bishop Charles E. Blake, I was shocked to see what was taking place in the inner-city and urban areas throughout the United States. Crack cocaine, gang violence, and AIDS were tragically snatching young African Americans from the streets, seemingly, at will. Unfortunately, the church was not exempt. Many of these individuals were the sons, daughters, and relatives of the members of West Angeles. There was at least one gang, AIDS, or drug related funeral at the church every week. The membership was over 16,000 at the time, and someone was always related, in some way, to the deceased.

Because of the frequency of the funerals, I became good friends with the funeral director and watched how he treated every family with such a natural compassion. I went to his new facility and was in awe. I had never seen a funeral home in the African American community that was so nice. It was first class with marble entries and gold trim. The celestial music playing in the immaculately clean lobby made you think you were approaching the pearly gates. Because of the circumstances behind many of the deaths, families needed earthly reassurance.

I discovered funerals have a way of bringing out the best or the worst in a person with little in between. During this time, family, friends, and neighbors demonstrate unbelievable kindness and compassion by cooking meals, delivering flowers, giving money, and speaking loving words. But, death, at its worst, is hell on earth. For example, mean words may be spoken to injure or defame the deceased. In turn, this causes a resentment for the disrespected beloved and the next thing you know retaliation occurs, and there is another dead body.

During a conversation with the funeral director, he talked about his unwelcomed success. He had gained tremendous wealth from the steady increase of deaths in the African American community. He conducted 6-10 funerals six days a week and over 50 percent were under the age of 40. There was a real sense of grief in his eyes as he shared.

Regretfully, the topic and area I felt least prepared to minister was continuously revisiting me. I watched Bishop Blake present masterful eulogies and console families as only a senior pastor could. His words were kind, reassuring, and supportive. I would see the same family members return to church weeks later and join because of his connection with them during their storm. I believe you always have a special connection with those you help through their storm.

A high number of the murders occurred on Crenshaw Blvd., which runs through South Central Los Angeles from the 10-Freeway dividing the Crips from the Bloods, two well-known gangs. Therefore, it was glorified in rap songs as the place to be. It is also the street which houses the West Angeles Church and all its properties. As a result, the Los Angeles Police Department (LAPD), would stop in frequently to give briefings to the church staff regarding gang activity in the area.

There were numerous occasions where gang members' caskets were shot at in churches or while at the funeral homes. One would never imagine that known gang members that were memorialized at churches or funeral homes in rival gang territory would be shot even while in their caskets. As a result, the LAPD would make their presence known at funerals to deter retaliations of high ranking gang members. There was no such thing as, "resting in peace" until you were in the ground. None of this made sense to me because nothing like this was happening in the late '70s and early '80s before I left home for college. Nothing I experienced at ORU had prepared me for this type of ministry. It hit home harder than I ever imagined. The teenagers at our church were very candid about their fears and anxiety.

We had a youth rally and a pizza party that was sponsored by our church. We invited the young people in the church to invite their friends who were not members of the church. Even though Judy and I were group leaders, we did not have all the answers. At that time, we had no children of our own, but we did have a relational connection with these young people. Because we were still young enough that we remembered the challenges of being a teenager and because of the state of the community, my wife and I were compelled to help.

Immediately, Judy and I got involved with the high school youth without hesitation. Judy helped direct the youth choir filled with gifted young people. The choir sang with a passion and energy that would bring young and old to their feet clapping and singing. Because there were four services on a Sunday, it allowed us to take Mondays off and recover. However, we were shocked by the incoming, Tuesday morning calls informing us of members that had been killed in a drive-by shooting. In one instance, a young, lively and energetic young man who had just sung in the choir on Sunday morning was shot and killed. He had no gang affiliation, no criminal record, and no known enemies. He was just sitting in the wrong car, in the wrong place, at the wrong time.

It was a wakeup call and no one was exempt from the L.A. gang warfare, not even *church kids* who were trying to do the right thing. I could not help but think, this was a storm that teenagers should not have to experience. Saying goodbye to a friend, brother, and choir mate had devastating emotional effects. Sadly, there was nothing in my education at ORU to draw from to help me minister to these kids. Therefore, I employed Dr. Carpenter's instruction. I met with the young people and I just listened. I provided a shoulder to cry on, and gave stern advice against retaliation. I let them vent, and I did not try to have all the answers. I did, however, know that God had all the answers. The challenge was conveying the message without sounding too *preachy* to these young minds who were in shock. I wanted to communicate the true essence of the gospel in a palatable way, and at the same time, recognize the pain and sense of loss these young kids were feeling.

The storm of death is unpredictable. You think you can project the forecast with pinpoint accuracy only to see it take a sharp turn, and rain down grief without any notice. This was the case in my own personal experience.

I had just picked up my son from school and was in the drive-thru line at Burger King. This was a part of our normal routine before going home to start on homework. I had just placed my order for large fries when the phone rang. "Hello! Mommy's sick!" was the high-pitched scream I heard.

I replied, "What do you mean Mommy's sick? What happened?" As my heart started to race, the phone was given to my mother's pastor, who I had known for over 30 years and his voice sounded shaken.

He still managed to tell me, "They think your mother has had a stroke. She is not talking and they are running some tests."

I managed to put a few questions together, "What hospital are you at? Does she have a good doctor? Where was she when this happened?" I had just spoken to her the day before and she was perfectly fine. As a matter of fact, she was coming to visit me the next week. I had already purchased her airline ticket. However, there was little additional information for them to give. When I hung up the phone, I was numb. As beads of sweat began to form on my forehead and the smell of french fries filled the car, I was shaken from my stupor by the women in the drive-thru window yelling, "Pay for the food and keep it moving!" After hearing the devastating news, I had no appetite and gave my food to my son, who could visibly see I was distraught. I immediately began making calls to my brother who lived a few blocks from me and made arrangements for us to be on a flight within eight hours. I lived a fast-paced life now and was accustomed to responding when the bell rung. It was now ringing for my Momma.

My brother and I arrived in Chicago, Illinois, by 11:00 a.m. the next morning, were in a rental car, and at the hospital within an hour. Ironically, we were at the same hospital where I was born. Although the environment was familiar, there were obvious upgrades over the past 40 years. New paint, floors, wing additions, were all a part of the hospital's *face lift*. Even with all the changes, I found the Intensive Care Unit (ICU). It was something about the sterile smell of the hospital when we got on the elevator that brought back the memories of being a patient in the hospital for over a month after being hit by a car at 16. I survived, and I was going to my mother's floor with the intentions of helping her survive.

We stepped off the elevator to a brightly lit floor and saw one of my sisters and several members of my mother's church in the family waiting room. We greeted everyone with cordial hugs, but I was on a mission to see my mother. I excused myself and started making my way to her room. The glass sliding doors opened and released with a gush of cool air as I entered the room. I needed it because I was not sure of what I would see. Short of a winter cold, I was not accustomed to seeing my mother sick. This was all new to me. She was a rock and pillar, who never got sick and took care of everyone else, when I would ask, "How are you feeling, Mom?" Her general response was always, "Tired." But, she would go and get her rest. Then, she would return with remarkable energy for an 80-year-old women.

But, now I was looking at a woman that appeared to be asleep. A respirator was assisting her with her breathing. The consistent humming sound of air being pushed into her lungs filled the room. At that moment, it was difficult to process everything that was happening. I felt overwhelmed by the entire experience. Even though she seemed peaceful, I could tell she was fighting for her life. I wanted to cheer her on with the words, "Fight Momma. Fight." But what was she fighting for? I inhaled the cool air of the room. Feeling helpless, I backed out of the room. I was not going to shed a tear. I was going to figure out a way to get her back on her feet with a great testimony of how she was healed.

As I backed out of the room, I slightly bumped into my brother who had followed me into the room without my knowledge. I could see he was also going through a range of emotions. Neither one of us knew how to respond after seeing Momma. We stepped into the hall together without speaking a word. My sister and my mother's pastor came to join us. Before we could speak any words, a young doctor in blue surgical scrubs appeared seemingly out of nowhere and said, "You must be Mrs. McAllister's family?"

My brother and I simultaneously responded, "Yes." My sister then introduced us to the Doctor that had been attending to my mother. He was a neurologist that specialized in treating stroke victims. The doctor explained that my mother had a massive stroke that was still bleeding. Unfortunately, the bleeding had produced a great deal of pressure on the brain and put my mother in a coma. According to the doctor, there were only two choices. We could agree that Momma go into surgery to stop the bleeding or we could wait and hope the bleeding stopped on its own. He then gave the caveat of my mother having a 50/50 chance of surviving the surgery, "Based on your mother's age, it would be a challenge for her to survive the surgery, but she definitely would never be the same. On the other hand, waiting to see if the bleeding would stop on its own would give her a much better chance of recovery to normalcy than having the surgery. Sadly, if the bleeding did not stop she would have more damage and there would be nothing we could do."

Clearly there were no good options. We needed a miracle. As I was nodding my head, pondering the decision that needed to be made, I looked up to see the Doctor and the rest of my family staring at me, waiting for me to respond. Before I responded to the stares, I asked a direct question to the doctor, "If this was your mother, what would you do"? You could tell he was not prepared for my response, but now all eyes were on him and not on me.

He began speaking in a stuttered tone, "I'm not really sure, but you have to consider carefully as it relates to your mother and the type of person she was before the stroke, compared to what she will be after the surgery. My mother is very active and would not want to be limited or be cared for continuously by others. I wouldn't operate on her."

"Let's wait and let God work a miracle," was our consensus as a family. The decision was made; we would wait overnight and hope for the best. Once the decision was made, there was some sense of relief. The waiting and anticipation game was now underway. Questions bombarded my mind, "Did we make the right decision? If we made the wrong decision, would the guilt overtake us? What will happen next"?

My oldest sister arrived in a whirlwind. She came in with energy and a take charge manner that let you know she had arrived and was going to make everything alright. I tried to prepare her for what she would see when she saw Momma. Sadly, she did not hear anything I said. She walked into the room and began calling Momma as if she was waking her from an afternoon nap. She spoke firm and directly, "Mommy! Mommy! Wake up!" She asked the question, "What did they give her?" There was no response at all from my mother. She continued for two to three minutes and then realized Momma was not waking up.

The next morning, I was at the hospital early to see a great miracle. I did not see any one, but the doctor had just come out of a conference room. He approached me with a solemn look on his face and he said, "The bleeding did not stop and it seems to have caused some severe damage. All we can do is make her comfortable." I was speechless and enraged all at the same time. I felt as though the doctor should have done something more to make my mother better. Instead, the doctor seemed nonchalantly disconnected, and unengaged. He had given up on my mother. I thought to myself, "Didn't he believe in God? Didn't he believe in miracles? We would show him."

At that moment, I went into my Momma's room and all I needed was a moment to show him what he had missed. Momma was not going out like this. I believed in God and I knew God worked miracles. That doctor was getting ready to see one. However, the moment I looked at my mother, I knew she was not going to wake up. She appeared almost the same as she did the day before, but something was missing. Momma's body now appeared like a shell, and all I could do was stare at what was left of her. I sat down in the chair where my brother had spent the night. When he returned, I told him what the doctor said and let him know I would spend the night with Momma. I did not want her to be alone when she transitioned from this life into the next life. Also, my brother needed a moment to digest the news.

Two days later, my mother was placed in hospice care and passed two days later. My wife and children came back with me for the funeral services, and we accepted the fact that our day had come. This was our season to experience the storm of death. What we did not know, however, was the intensity of the storm.

I thought we could manage the storm of death by staying busy and keeping a sense of normalcy. Nothing was normal because I could no longer expect to hear the familiar voice say, "Hello," when I dialed the first phone number I had learned by heart. There was no normalcy when I walked into the empty home of my childhood. The normalcy was further shattered when my wife received a call that her mother was in the final stages of her battle with cancer. She questioned, "What did they mean by *final stages*?" She was told, "You should come home as soon as possible." She shared the gravity of the situation with me and I was certain this could not be happening.

We had just held home-going services two days earlier for my Mom, and now my wife's mother was possibly in the last few days of her life. It was hard for me to focus and comfort my wife because I was still grieving the sudden death of my mother. This lingering visitation of death was a real storm. It just would not pass. It was like a rain cloud that settled over my family and dumped everything it had. It was not a light rain; it was the kind of rain that stung your skin with its force.

My mother in-law was extremely kind and caring. I would sit and listen to guys talk about their mother in-laws like they were fanatics. In stark contrast, my mother in-law was angelic. There were times when she would speak poetic words of wisdom with a soft West Indian accent that could rock you to sleep. Then she would break out in laughter to let you know not to take her or life so seriously. Unfortunately, like my mother, my mother-in-law was gone. The call came at midday from my wife that my mother-in-law had taken her last breath and was no longer suffering from the viciousness of cancer she had battled for the past seven years. I asked my wife how she was doing and she responded, "I had the honor to be by my mother's side when she transitioned into the next life to let her know it was okay to go."

We all know the day will come when our parents will die and no matter how we try to brace ourselves for it, we are never prepared. The other dimension is no one ever thinks about losing two parents within 10 days and planning funeral services back to back. In this case, there was no time to recover. We were knocked down again and punch drunk by the blows of death. Needless to say, my perspective on death and how to handle it was changed in more ways than imagined. The words I shared with others in the past now had taken on personal meaning. I had to practice what I preached. I was now much more compassionate to the losses of loved ones by others. I was now a member of a unique group of survivors that had survived the storm of parental death. I recognize how blessed and fortunate I was to survive two deaths less than 10 days apart. What I discovered was many have not survived similar storms.

Daughters have found themselves paralyzed, emotionally and relationally, by the loss of the first and only man that ever loved them unconditionally, *daddy*. In some instances, sons are filled with guilt because of the stress of their rebellious lives which may have shortened momma's life. These sons realized that whether they were in jail or the slow little guy on the football field, momma was always their cheerleader and made them feel loved. She would sit and listen to stories that did not make sense when others were no longer interested. But now momma was gone.

These sons and daughters retreat into addictions to anesthetize the pain caused by guilt, shame, and unimaginable grief. Alcohol, sleeping pills, narcotics, unhealthy relationships, and even food become the comforts to help them cope. These elements can cause even more storms. The valley of the shadow of death is real and can cause you to have an unimaginable fear. We can have a confidence that leads us through this valley of despair and brings a healing that is unimaginable and not even expected. It is called time. Time will bring healing to the days of grief caused by death. When we allow time to saturate our wounded hearts with the power of love and pleasant memories, we can experience the calm after the storm.

The Walking Dead

One night, one decision, and one hit would change one girl's dream into a never-ending nightmare. How could Candace know that the words, "I will take you places you have never been," would lead her down a spiraling path straight into the belly of the *hell*, addiction?

Oftentimes in response to life storms, drug addiction becomes a quick remedy, or a way of coping. Unfortunately, drug addiction allows one to escape from one storm to an even worse self-inflicted storm. It is likened to when a ship is out to sea, facing the threat of a storm and the captain creates holes in the hull of the ship, causing a greater anticipation of sinking. Decisions between vital resources and human survival are necessary. Often, the weight of water, food and fuel can be the demise and destruction of the ship. However, now that you have preserved your method of transportation, how will you preserve your life? How do you move forward? What is the collateral damage from throwing your necessities overboard to keep the ship from sinking? This is the quandary Candace found herself in the day I encountered her while on my patrol.

Candace

The 6:00 p.m. to 2:00 a.m. swing shift exposes LAPD officers to the busiest call times. This evening was no exception. Rush hour had just ended, and the sun was setting and giving the last bit of an orange glow on a fall day in Los Angeles. You could tell it was fall because the sun took its last breath of dispensed light; and then the temperatures dropped like a paratrooper invading a foreign land.

I was rolling up the window of my 1990 Caprice Classic police issued squad car. It was the last time the faithful Chevy would be used. The Ford Crown Victoria, the new black and white police cars, were considered more appropriate and dependable for policing L.A. As I approached the intersection of Washington Blvd. and Hauser, traffic was much slower than normal. It did not take long to see that the *walking dead* were out early.

The section on Washington Blvd. between La Brea Ave. and Hauser Blvd. contained the *walking dead* of the 90's. Before it was popularized 20 years later in a television series, I had an opportunity, night after night, to watch those that had abandoned themselves to walking the streets to find their next hit of heroin, share the glass pipe of rock cocaine, or just put anything they could find in a needle for pleasure. Some of the people who walked these streets were the by-products of what happens when smoking a rock of cocaine for the first time, for fun, turns into a brutal game of *chasing the rock*. A person chasing the rock intensely craves for another hit of the crack pipe and will do anything to satisfy the consuming urge.

From a distance, I did not recognize Candace. As traffic began to slow, I was only focused on hitting my siren to move traffic along. With total disregard for my presence, Candace was defiant and continued working the intersection as I passed. Curiously, I watched in my rear-view mirror as she waved a car around the corner. My Chevy engine roared as I whipped a U-turn and simultaneously turned on the police lights. The car that Candace was approaching began to pull off slowly. For the moment, I just let the car go. I turned off the flashing lights so the rubbernecking would not start and cause traffic to continue to slow.

At the present time, I had not decided if I was going to arrest this woman, write her a ticket, or give a warning. As I approached, I could see stains on her light sheer clothing. She rolled her glassy eyes that were protruding from her sunken, grayish, brown skin. It would be an understatement to say she was *unkept*. The condition of her hair, clothes, and personal hygiene revealed she had stopped caring a while ago. Before I could catch myself, "Candace, is that you?" were the first words that came out of my mouth.

When Candace realized who I was, she dropped her head in shame. At the same time, she looked down at the ground as if she was looking for a hole to bury herself. I did not recognize Candace as one of the regular prostitutes I had seen on the streets. Candace was my neighbor. She lived three doors down from me with her grandmother. However, the last time I saw Candace was about two years earlier on a corner in her school uniform.

It seemed like yesterday, when I saw Candace on a corner waiting for the bus to take her to the private prep school she attended in West L.A. Everyone in the neighborhood looked out for her because her Grandmother was from the South and emphasized good manners, such as, "Yes Ma'am. No Sir." She was the poster child of perfection, and the pride of her grandmother's heart. I personally would have protected her like my own daughter. Unfortunately, the angelic glow that once radiated from her caramel skin tone was now faded, her distinct large oval eyes were cloudy, and Candace was now a shadow of her former self. I thought to myself, "This could not be the same person I saw two years ago."

In a state of disbelief, I asked her what happened. I had to hear her story. I reassured her that I was not trying to arrest her, but I was sincerely concerned about her and how she had managed to get in this condition. Even though the streets had obviously aged her, she reverted to a 12-year-old as the tears began to stream down her face. I listened to her mumble through two years of her young world being turned upside down. It all started when she went to her high school prom with the wrong person, one of the boys from *the block.*

Candace went to a girls' prep school that was predominantly white, with upper middle class students. Because she was an excellent student, she had earned a scholarship to the University of Southern California (USC). Although she was well liked, she received no attention from the boys that visited the school. So, when it came time for the prom, Candace picked the wrong guy. When she called his name, and who he was affiliated with, I knew everyone she had mentioned was gang banging and selling dope.

As Candace recanted the events of that night, she was visibly distraught. Candace's date thought her prom was boring and almost got into a fight with some white boys that were staring at him. As a result, he convinced Candace to leave the prom and go to a house party in their neighborhood. He manipulated her by telling Candace she needed to learn how to kick it with her own people. It was at the party, Candace had her first experience with rock cocaine. Under the auspicious that it would relax Candace and allow her to enjoy the party, her date offered her a hit. Although she initially refused, the pressure of wanting to be *cool* won her over.

The next thing Candace remembered after smoking the rock was waking up in some hotel room alone. The beautiful prom dress her grandmother bought her was nowhere to be found. To make matters worse, when she stepped out of the hotel into the bright LA sunshine, she looked back at the clock in the room to see it was one o'clock in the afternoon. While shaking her head, she told me that her grandmother had given her two hours past her 10:00 p.m. curfew and now she was going to have to face her more than 12 hours late.

A blank stare came over Candace as she continued to tell her story. "When I got home, my grandmother looked at me and said, Get out!"

"I was planning to travel, work some for the summer, start USC, and eventually go to law school." Even though Candace's speech was slightly slurred, you could tell—at some point in her life—she was well educated. Candace continued her story, "My grandmother finally let me back in the house and then told me how she did not want me to end up like my mother." Candace's mother died young. It was never clear to me how she died, but it sounded like Candace's grandmother believed it was preventable and was determined not to let Candace go down the same path.

In our conversation, Candace did most of the talking and I mainly listened. After about 15 minutes, another police car came up to check on me. I waived my fellow officer off with a code four, LAPD code for no assistance needed. Candace continued by explaining that she hooked up one more time with her former prom date, because he convinced her they had a good time.

Candace could not remember anything, but she thought she would try the rock one more time. This time, she felt everything. Before she knew it, Candace was giving the best part of herself to a man she did not love, and a drug that stirred an insatiable craving. To escalate the situation, Candace found herself wanting the *rock* more than she wanted sex. However, her *friend* would not give her another rock unless she had sex with him. This began a downward spiral and destructive cycle for Candace. Her body became the means by which she was able to maintain her high. Eventually, Candace began to sleep with complete strangers to satisfy the craving for the *rock*. She was *turned out*. For the next three days, she engaged in a sex and drug binge.

When she finally came out of the crack house, she stumbled back home and beat on the door. When Candace's grandmother answered the door, it was at that moment Candace realized she had missed her graduation. There was no explaining, Candace could tell her grandmother was heartbroken. She left three days earlier with the hopes of getting a job to take care of herself until school started at USC. Unfortunately, Candace worked at the Taco Bell for two weeks before going on her binge and losing any hopes of a scholarship. She never went to USC.

After a year on the streets and living with *friends*, Candace made up her mind she was going to *get herself together*. This was one of the countless times she said she would never do drugs again. With a strong determination, she went back to her grandmother's house to live. Sadly, Candace's grandmother had a stroke and died three months earlier. Unfortunately, they could not find Candace, who was on one of her sprees. Candace said she could not access the house because it was on the market. I remember passing by Candace's grandmother's house wondering what happened to them. I had no recollection of the house being up for sale. The mystery was finally unfolding before me, in a heartbreaking story of this young lady drowning in the raging storm of drug addiction.

Riddled by the continuous guilt of possibly causing her grandmother's death and losing all her hopes and dreams, she had now joined the *walking dead*. She was too young to die, but it was evident that everything in her had aged beyond her true years. But, to satisfy my own curiosity, I asked Candace how old she was. Unfortunately, she confirmed my fears. She was only 19. I was now looking at a 19-year-old who was educated and had incredible dreams of a promising future. However, gone were the long pretty braids with perfectly straight parts. All I could see was natural hair creeping out from under a matted wig, and skin that was speckled and scarred from feeding off the toxic combinations of whatever was used to rock up her crack cocaine.

Candace's pain was deep from her losses. What started as an experiment to have a little fun was a full-blown, uncontrollable, drug addiction that had unmercifully ravaged her life. The soiled, greyed mini skirt she was wearing revealed nothing attractive. The pretty white smile from the bus stop was now replaced with yellow teeth that were shamefully covered with a thin frail hand, and burnt finger tips.

As I stood there feeling compassion for Candace, who could very well have been my own daughter, I thought to myself, "She would have to find some place to stay for the night because it would be in the 50's tonight." Even so, that was nothing compared to the chill I felt that night regarding her future. I was no longer in the mode of police officer. I had an overwhelming concern for this young lady who came to the crossroads of life and chose the wrong path. She had thrown overboard many of the vital resources needed for survival.

I wanted to help, but had no idea where to start. I asked myself, "Is her life really over at 19?" She was in the grips of an addiction that was holding her like super glue, and at the rate she was going, she would not last any longer than a year. Her life demonstrated all the signs of becoming a statistic of a drug overdose or contracting AIDS and dying prematurely.

I had attended funerals of congregants' family members that had died this way, but I never knew their story or saw their rapid downward spiral. After about five minutes of silence, Candace stared into the night without any sense of purpose. The silence was broken when she said in a familiar voice that I remembered from years past, "Officer Mac, can I go now?"

"Where are you going"? I replied.

She stumbled to find words, "I don't know. I'll just go home," she said hesitatingly.

"Where is home?"

"I got a spot."

It was clear that her spot was the *streets*, or wherever she could find to lay her head. I gave her the usual kind words I am sure were familiar, "Take care of yourself and get some help." She had created the never-ending storm of addiction. As far as Candace was concerned, there was no way out of her life that was driven by her addiction. Consequently, Candace was not only in a storm, but she was also feeling like she had been tossed overboard as discarded cargo. She was trying to float, but the waves of life had taken their toll. The look in her eyes showed there was no more fight left. In Candace's mind, she had nothing to fight for, no one to cheer her on, no one who seemed to care if she lived or died, no one who would miss her; and ultimately, she had no one to tell her there was something to live for. So, Candace was hopeless.

Just as Candace turned to walk away, I broke protocol and told her that she had to fight. I forgot about the uniform and the badge that I was wearing. During my police academy training, I was instructed to never take a personal interest in anyone or anything. Taking a personal interest resulted in taking the job home, sleepless nights, a messiah complex, and, ultimately, a shortened career.

I knew Candace did not need to hear a sermon because she knew the difference between right and wrong. She knew she had brought most of what she was experiencing on herself. I did not need to tell her that she knew better. In contrast, Candace needed to hear she could be better. My training as a minister could have given her a lot of biblical metaphors and scripture that she may have understood, but most likely would not have been useful for Candace at this moment. In this moment, what Candace needed was a miracle, and the demonstration of the love we often preach. I could not just watch Candace walk away, so I simply said, "Candace, you can't and you don't have to keep living like this."

She stopped as she was walking away and stood with her back to me. In that moment, Candace broke down. I saw the rising and falling of her shoulders through the sheer black blouse she was wearing. She was heaving and crying uncontrollably. I wanted to call my wife because Candace needed someone to just hold her. It was totally inappropriate for me to even approach her but, I could not just let her walk away. I believe when someone has fallen overboard, you should grab them if you can and hold on for dear life.

I continued to talk to Candace as she had her back turned to me. I told her again, "Baby girl, you can make it if you try. God loves you and your grandmother would want you to show that you can fight. Fight for her, fight for yourself, fight for the purpose that God has for your life."

At that moment, one of Candace's *walkers* came around the corner and saw her. He looked at me and thought Candace was crying because she was being arrested. He started trying to plead her case. She told him that she was good. He kept moving because he probably was carrying the next hit her body craved. He was also motivated to keep moving because another police car came around the corner. I was glad to see it was my division partner.

She was a lady that went beyond anyone's expectation of a Los Angeles Police officer. The best way to describe her would be a cross between Oprah and Patti Labelle. She was short and stout and hated getting out of the car. She knew the policy and procedures extremely well and should have been a sergeant, but made it clear she was not going to *baby sit* grown folks with guns. She walked over to me shaking her head in disgust.

"You done made this girl cry out here preaching to her," were the first words out of her mouth. She had a sense of humor that could bring levity to the most serious and depressing situations. "Hey baby, did he mess up your work for tonight? I'll make him let you go, but you got to get off the street. I'll listen to him for you."

Just like that, Candace went from tears to laughter. "She's funny," was her reply. Like magic, Deb started talking to her and had an immediate connection. Within five minutes, Candace was in Deb's Police car and on her way to a rehab shelter for women. I followed them about three miles to the building in a cheap part of downtown L.A.

I said a prayer to myself as Deb walked Candace into the two-story building. As she was disappearing through the doors, I extended an invitation to Candace to come to the church. She said she would. As we went back to the car, Deb started cursing at me and making it clear she was not Mother Teresa. This went on for about five minutes. The truth was, Deb had one of the most tender hearts you could find on the streets. She never expressed it because she also knew the rules of not getting personally involved. She made the exception because she saw me making the exception.

Deb said to me, "You can't save the world. These folks out here are going to do what they want." I began to tell Deb why I had taken an interest in Candace. Deb stopped me and told me about her niece that she had buried last year. She did not sound optimistic that Candace would make it, but she wanted to try. Initially, we had planned to go out to dinner. However, we no longer had a taste for food at all. Instead, we met two of our cars that were working in our division and just had a cup of coffee. I never saw Candace on the streets again, but I saw numerous others that went down the spiraling abyss of drug addiction. I am not sure what their demons were and what induced their addiction, but the toll addiction took on the lives of people was difficult to watch.

There was no respect of persons. I watched famous actors, athletes, politicians, and yes, even preachers, battle addictions of all sorts. I watched some fighting for their lives, and taking it one step and one day at a time. Some won and some lost, but all I know is they were in a fight for their life. They had thrown many of their dreams, gifts, and talents overboard just to find out they survived the initial storm and would need them. Unfortunately, they could not dive in the cruel waters of life to get them back. The amazing thing about real survivors is they find new resources to sustain life. They find hope, fulfillment, a new perspective, and a greater appreciation for the little things previously taken for granted. Real survivors take pride in the opportunity to just have a second chance. The pain of making sacrifices and the patience of waiting provide new fuel to energize and propel a survivor into destiny. A true survivor rejects addictions as counterfeit revenue and refocuses on the resources that assist in forward progress.

Blindsided

Country music was not my favorite, but I was now surrounded by a community who, lived, loved, and breathed country music since we had moved to Nashville, Tennessee. Gasping for breath, I watched as my phone vibrated and flashed on the elliptical in front of me. Technically, I was still on duty. But, as a habit I kept my phone close. As the machine slowed, I wiped the sweat from my forehead and answered the phone. What came next would initiate the greatest storm of my life.

"Hello", the voice on the end was short and no nonsense. "Darin, I need you to come into the office this evening." It was my supervisor's graveled voice. He always sounded like he was just waking up from a deep sleep.

"Sure, be there in 30 minutes."

Annoyed by the fact that I would miss the beginning of the playoff basketball game between the Lakers and Phoenix, I quickly made my way to the office. I was clueless to the notion that in the next 30 minutes my entire life would take a 180 degree turn. I could not have fathomed that the very *justice* I fought for, would now fight against me.

As I stepped off the elevator, I was greeted at the door by familiar faces who now had removed ties worn earlier in the day. Everyone, including me, seemed bothered by having to come in after hours. I quickly realized, I was the guest of honor. The long mahogany rectangle table, where I was asked to sit, still smelled of dusting oil from the afternoon cleaning, and my pleasant smile was met with cold responses, and averting eyes. In a hush voice, the Special Agent in Charge, an African America woman, blindsided me with the words that would change my life forever, "Darin, you have been indicted."

Of course, I believed I was being pranked and this was a terrible, sophisticated joke that would cause everyone to burst into laughter at any moment. Unfortunately, no one *cracked*. Instead, suddenly all the air was sucked out of the room. I literally found myself as breathless as I had been 30 minutes earlier at the gym. Reluctantly, one of my, now former peers, slid an official document across the table. The words, *United States of America Vs. Darin Lee McAllister*, seemed to jump off the front page of a book-like document. I had seen and served documents of this nature on several occasions. It was official. As my mind raced, I turned the pages to verify the seals and judgments. As this point, the Special Agent in Charge's words, "I'm sorry," seemed empty and vague.

Afterwards, I was escorted from the conference room, through the cubicles, and into my supervisor's office. Upon entering, "Is your gun on you?" were the first words out of his mouth. Being meticulously trained to observe my surroundings, I noticed to the rear of my right side an armed agent cautiously watching my every move.

"It's in my car," I replied.

"Let me have the keys." I set the keys on his desk. I watched silently and hopelessly as he picked them up and handed them to another agent who came up from behind me. In a non-emotional tone, my supervisor said, "Do you have your creds?" In a state of shock, I reached inside my sports coat pocket and removed the gold badge I had received 16 years earlier. It was in a customized black leather wallet I had purchased along with the specially laminated credentials bearing the picture taken of me on the fifth day of being at the FBI academy. As I placed my FBI credentials on my supervisor's desk, I questioned his ability to be so matter of fact. He looked away as if he was being pulled in another direction.

He nodded his head and two other supervisors came up and said, "Come on, Darin let's clean out your desk and get your personal items."

My first thought was, "There's nothing I want from that desk." However, when I turned the corner, I saw the picture of my wife and individual pictures of my children in wooden frames from their younger years. Up until now, I was in shock and felt no emotions. However, seeing my wife and children caused heat to begin to rise from the pit of my stomach. The churning in my gut that began like the warming of a campfire was now transitioned to a volcano rumbling with hot lava. But, I refused to break.

Mechanically, I began opening the drawers and pulling out trinkets that had been picked up over my 16 years as a FBI

Special agent. I found myself grabbing things that seem of little importance: a coffee cup from Desert Storm, patches from the various task forces, paperweights from the Los Angeles Office, hats, and t-shirts I had stuffed in the bottom file-cabinet drawer. Feeling as empty as the cardboard, toilet paper box, and the plastic mail-bin handed to me by my supervisor, I placed my personal belongings in the box and bin.

As I gathered various items and pictures, memories of the last 16 years flooded my mind. Everything from major arrests of bank robbers and fugitives to retirements and Christmas parties was now at the forefront of my mind. In contrast, the pictures were reflecting happier times than what I was currently experiencing. What seemed like eternity, was less than an hour. My hard work and dedication of 16-years was over in less than an hour, and to this day, I have never seen anyone in that room again.

The normalcy of home helped to comfort the conflicting emotions. Fortunately, the next day was the last day of school, so everyone wanted to stay up late and play games. While the children played, I called my wife into the bedroom and tried to find words to express to her what was happening to me...to us. Before I could speak a word, my heart began to race and I found myself grasping for air again. She saw the rare moment that I was visibly shaken and could not put words together to form a sentence. She grabbed my hand and asked what happened. Again, before I could put my words together, and through the tears, I mumbled, "I've been indicted."

Although I had no idea how she would react. Her response was calm and stable. Judy comforted me with an unimaginable strength. Out of the silence, Judy began to pray. Because of my state of mind and the overwhelming emotions, I could not hear or process every word that was spoken, but when I heard *amen*, I felt the peace of God enter my mind and my heart. Looking me in the eyes, Judy spoke the words that would carry us through the next few years, "This is much bigger than us and God is going to see us through."

After waking up the next morning from what I had hoped was a bad dream, I was quickly awakened into reality when the phone began to ring with anonymous phone calls from reporters. My wife was bombarded with intruding and cruel questions. To add to the chaos, internet stories started appearing, and our address was now common knowledge. With the publishing of the news, I fully expected news trucks on our front lawn at any moment with satellite antennas popping up like dandelions. However, the first sign of distress came when the words appeared in a news article, *Gospel Singer Judith Christie-McAllister's husband arrested for wire fraud.*

With the unfolding events of the morning, the reality struck me, this would not be a private issue to be resolved and quietly settled. It was going to become very public, and worst of all, humiliate the woman I love and cherish. The false accusations would not stop with me; she would experience guilt by association. Her integrity and character would be questioned without cause. She would have to experience the silencing of a room when she walked in because all previous conversations were about her. The publicity forced us to sit down with our children before they left for school. I did not want my children to suffer or be distracted in any way, so I sat down, and made an attempt to explain to them that even though this was their last day of school, some of their friends or teachers may make comments about me that were false. I felt a sense of relief that it was the last day of school. All they had to do was make it until noon and then they would be out for the summer.

In another attempt to manage the crises, I started contacting my closest friends. I wanted them to hear the truth from me, before hearing it second hand or sensationalized media spins. It was now almost 8:30 a.m. in Los Angeles, and I knew the first person I had to contact was Bishop Charles Blake, the man I knew as Father and Pastor. After my own Father died, I had given him that place in my life. In keeping with the relationship, I had with my natural father, I considered myself a problem-free child. Now, how was I going to explain to him what was happening? He answered the phone with a jovial, "What does the FBI need me for this early in the morning?" followed by spontaneous laughter. This was our norm, only things were not normal.

As bad as I wanted to keep the moment light I could not contain myself. I started having a panic attack and I could not get the words out to say, "I've been indicted." My voice cracked as if I was going through puberty. With a second feeble attempt, what was a single tear running down my face had now turned into a stream, causing my vision to blur. "Bishop, I have been indicted for wire fraud." There was about a five second pause and he shifted to a concerned and compassionate dad, wanting to know how Judy and I were doing. He instinctively spoke words of encouragement and support. He made himself available if any additional assistance or counsel was needed. Without pause, he began to pray and I began to weep. I had heard similar prayers prayed for others at funerals and various crises. I never imagined I would also require the same prayers.

I placed several additional calls. My best friend was ready to get on the next plane headed to Nashville. The other call was to meet with a local pastor, Bishop Joseph Walker. He cleared his schedule and invited me to his home where he spoke life into me. Every one of these men gave me the strength to know I could make it through the day. I knew if I could make it through the day, I could make it through the week, and then through the month. It would be one day at a time.

It took several months for the initial shock to subside with a daily commitment not to give into the temptations to have a pity party. The word of God had to become a reality and not just words on a page. Although, I was raised in the church and earned a Bachelor of Arts in theology, the words were coming alive in ways I had yet to discover.

While contrasting similar discoveries with the likes of John Newton, all words were now viewed in the contexts of my current experience. Newton's experience of being out to sea on his slave ship caused him to place a divine S.O.S. He placed this S.O.S before the S.O.S code had even been invented in the practical sense. He placed his S.O.S directly to God when his slave ship was battered by angry waves and appeared as if it would sink at any moment. After experiencing what he believed was a divine intervention at sea, Newton converted to Christianity and became an Evangelical Cleric, abandoning the slave trade. He went a step further and became one of Britain's strongest abolitionists. His experience led him to author the song, *Amazing Grace.* The truth of God's grace, through the song, came alive with a power to transcend culture, politics, and prejudice — because, at some point, grace is a necessity in everyone's life.

I took a stand to fight what I was accused of based on the grace I had received and the truths I knew. I understood the legal system and how it worked because I had been a part of it for over 20 years. I could have given in and made a deal to avoid a trial. Everyone involved likes to do this because it is easier. I had advised numerous individuals to not confess to something they did not do and most did not unless they were coerced. A plea deal would be the biggest lie told. I would have to manipulate the system for lesser punishment and tell a lie. Make a statement that I knowingly and intentionally did something that I did not do. Within 6 months, I was in trial.

With a great sense of urgency, I began looking for legal representation. I knew a lot of attorneys, but very few were well versed in the Federal system. The few that were knowledgeable and available would be expensive. In my first consultation, I had an initial sense of relief.

The middle-aged attorney warmly invited me into his office that was modestly decorated with cheap motel paintings and outdated colors. He had stacks of papers and legal briefs on his long organized chaotic desk. His suit was a cheap polyester blend and his shoes looked like they were an orthopedic special. However, he was highly recommended and was labeled as being law enforcement friendly. He was experienced in defending law enforcement officers involved in bad shootings or misconduct while on duty. "So tell me what happened here and let me see if I can help you," were his no non-sense words. After ten minutes in his office, it sounded like someone gave him a scripted question to ask me, "Who did you piss off?" I had no idea how to respond because I did not think I had made any real enemies in Nashville.

The second attorney I met had won a case against the FBI and exposed an Agent that I knew very well for possible perjury. He was good and he knew he was good. When I sat in the soft leather chairs in his well-decorated office, I could not help but notice the plaques and accolades that were clearly displayed on the faux painted walls. He asked me three direct questions in rapid-fire session and then concluded with, "Who did you piss off?"

Both attorneys got the essence of the case within minutes and believed it was winnable and I was a credible witness for my defense. They acknowledged it would not be easy and apologized for what I was experiencing. Then they got to the reason they were in business. One quote was $60,000.00 for a retainer without a trial and the other was $100,000 if they began filing motions to dismiss. Considering I had filed for bankruptcy within the past 12 months, I was in no position to even negotiate with them. I had nothing to negotiate. Consequently, my fate would be in the hands of the public defender's office.

My attorneys knew my faith in God, and I lived it out in front of them. It was not a show or courthouse religion. I had read every scripture I could on faith and trusting God. I was excited to see how God was going to vindicate me. I was certain he was going to defeat my enemies and give me the victory. I expected my mourning to turn into dancing, and the enemy would return everything I lost a hundred-fold. I expected complete vindication and restoration. That is how every story of faith is supposed to go, right?

My New Best Friend

Ready! Set! Go! My heart was off to the races, but I was not running and my body was barely moving. Something about having to sit down and talk to my new court appointed attorney, triggered this uncontrollable pounding like horses on the home stretch of the Kentucky Derby on the inside of my chest.

My lead attorney was in his late thirties and had a calming demeanor. If I was profiling him from my previous experience with the Bureau, he would have been categorized as the *happy go lucky, good ole boy, politically correct conservative* who believed in justice for all. His Southern drawl was clear when he extended his hand and said, "Adam Grace, I'm so sorry about what has happened to you. I hope I can get you out of this mess. You must have really pissed someone off." I was beginning to hear a pattern, from multiple sources, that there was *someone* out there who did not like me. At least, that is what every one of these attorneys led me to believe.

Adam offered me a cup of coffee in his home office, and there I sat in this comfortable office that took up the entire first floor. The home looked like it was probably built in the 40's or 50's and had been restored to its original condition with a few minor upgrades for electrical. The dining room had been converted to a conference room with country chic decorations, and the first-floor bedroom was being used as an office for his assistant.

As I listened to Adam's simple selection of words and his young *Mr. Rogers* tone, I believed he would have an instant connection with the Tennessee locals. "I've reviewed your case and I see how this happened. Heck, I could have done the same thing. Let's see what they have. You have been in court plenty of times, so you can help review the discovery and make sure they aren't holding anything back. It looks like they gave us everything on a disc to go through." The initial plan sounded great. Then, five minutes later in walks a middle aged white woman who was out of breath and slightly apologetic for her tardiness. "Darin, this is Wendy Dawson. She will be assisting me on your case."

I extended my hand, and with a matter of fact response, she said, "Hello." Even though it was the beginning of June, her greeting was as cold as her freezing hands. We sat down and she quietly stared at me as if she was trying to read me from the inside out. Adam summarized what he knew about my case and asked if I was committed to going to trial. I listened as he explained my options and gave his opinion on the result. I was familiar with how things went with negotiating charges. I had a 19-count indictment that sounded horrible on the surface. But, when you examined what I was being charged with, it all centered around the one loan application that was used for every loan I received for income property.

If I was acquitted of one count, I would be acquitted of all the accounts. Unfortunately, it worked the same in reversed. If I was convicted of one, I would be convicted of all. The indictments were inseparable. The other three counts were thrown in to support like and similar conduct: two false information statements on my bankruptcy and the false information on a line of credit. Once everything was dissected and explained, Adam believed it was winnable, but Wendy finally spoke up when Adam left the room to take another call.

"This does not make sense to me. You seem to be a pretty smart guy with the FBI and all," she said with a real sense of sarcasm. "How could you do something like this? You expect people to believe this was just a mistake?" I was totally blindsided by her words. I felt as if I was being scolded by my 3rd grade teacher. Although I was much calmer now than I was in 3rd grade, I was beginning to wonder if she was experiencing inward conflict where my case was concerned. She had piercing blue eyes that were attempting to look at my soul rather than listen to the words that were coming out of my mouth. "You cannot get away with this. You told the bank that you made a half-million dollars a year and now say it was a mistake." This lady was going for the jugular; I had to fight back.

"I didn't tell anyone that I made a half-million dollars a year at any point in my life. My mistake was being unaware that I was signing an application at closing that stated I made a half million dollars that year when it was placed in front of me four years later."

Wendy paused and took a deep breath. There was a silence in the room that left me thinking who would make the next move. She inhaled and began firing again. "You are not believable! Why were you living in a million-dollar home? How much were you making as a FBI agent that made you think you could afford a million-dollar home?" At this point, she had pushed my button. She was obviously implying I was a corrupt agent who had obtained money by some illegal means to buy my home.

Now, I found myself in a position of defending myself. Although I felt offended by the insinuations I answered in a calm, but direct manner as I began to narrate my story, "I had no intention of purchasing a million-dollar home when my wife, our son, and two daughters moved to Tennessee. Originally, we had purchased land in a new subdivision for half that amount, so our home was being built. When we arrived in Tennessee, the foundation to our new home had just been poured. Then, without notice, I was told the project manager working on our home, quit. At this point, I began to feel pressure at the thought of my family being in an apartment over the holidays, and my son sleeping on the couch was already nagging at me." Despite Wendy's disinterested state and look of disbelief, I continued to tell my story. "The home my wife and I purchased was below the market asking price and was purchased as an investment with every intent to sell it after two years. When we tried to sell it, the market was already failing and we received few offers." Wendy nodded her head, but was still unsympathetic.

In fact, her next words were shocking. "I know I may seem like I am giving you a hard time, but this is nothing compared to what a prosecutor and jury are going to put you through. They are not going to like the fact that you were spending all this money on houses and real estate. I just want you to be prepared for much worse than I can give you." I was a little slow, but it clicked. Wendy was setting me up and trying to get an emotional reaction out of me. It was not by coincidence, but Wendy was now going to become my *new best friend*. We were truly the odd couple. She had no children, but she had a motherly approach. She also corrected me like a big sister who did not want to be embarrassed by a little brother.

Adam returned and dived into the conversation with, "Have you guys had a chance to talk? I apologize. I had to take that call. I stepped out because your partners from the FBI did not do a good job on a case they have against another one of my clients." I smiled because I was now on the other side getting a different perspective. Often, most defense attorneys did not believe FBI agents did satisfactory case work. Frequently, even though the cases against clients were weak, for some reason the defense attorneys always tried to work out a plea agreement. Just as I was thinking these thoughts to myself, the next words from Adam were surprisingly familiar. "Are you interested in working out a plea agreement? You could probably end up with just probation."

Without hesitation, I emphatically replied, "No, I'm not interested!" It was at that moment, Adam and Wendy knew the thought of a plea agreement was non-negotiable.

We spent the rest of the afternoon writing out a strategy. Wendy took meticulous notes and questioned everything as if I was already in front of a jury. What seemed like a week's worth of work had only been three hours. Although I was drained and physically exhausted, Wendy sent me home with plenty of homework. As a matter of fact, everyone had a list of things to do. Although my list seemed like it was the longest, I was not complaining. I realized I was in a fight for my life.

Time seemed to fly and just four months later, we were down to the wire. Our team had grown to eight now. A private investigator, a handwriting expert, a mortgage specialist, a legal assistant, and a comforting white Labrador who calmed us all when we were stressed.

Our private investigator confirmed most of the information I had told Adam. This gave Adam more confidence in what I was telling him. Our private investigator confirmed that my loan officer had been fired from the bank and had a history of falsifying loan documents. He had even taken a loan out in his mother in-law and brother's name without their knowledge.

The handwriting expert reviewed over ten years of my hand writing samples. She concluded that the loan applications the bank manager testified to the grand jury were completed by me were not in my handwriting. The private investigator also discovered the loan officer and the bank manager had a personal romantic relationship. Adam was excited about this information and seemed much more optimistic about going to trial.

Now, no team is complete without a member like Gary. Gary was from Texas and like everything in Texas, he was bigger than life. He had an infectious laugh and knew what he knew better than anyone on the planet. After reviewing the applications and the grand jury testimony, he was clearly convinced that I did not commit a crime and this case was a witch hunt and complete waste of the justice system's time and money. It felt good to have some folks to see the truth.

We met for several weeks in Adam's country home office. I was seeing something forming that I thought was exclusive to my time spent in the FBI. There was a bond forming that brought conversations about everything, but my case. The same thing happened at my FBI roundtables with my fellow agents. An hour was spent on sports and politics and about 20 minutes on the cases we were working. I remembered the early lectures I heard about warnings against the discussion of politics and religion to ensure the formation of long-lasting friendships. Well, the reality is that you learn more about someone and their true character and beliefs when you hear them talk about politics and religion.

I was used to adapting to the environment of being the only African American in the room. So, I made myself small and listened carefully to the passion that went into certain statements that were made about our new African American president that had been elected, President Barak Obama. There was clear questioning of President Obama's policies, but no real ability to make comparisons because there had never been an African American president prior to him. It was clear that Adam was not a Democrat, which he used as his fundamental reason for rejecting President Obama. It was better than possibly being tagged a racist. He was a liberal republican that had not bought into the hardline traditions of the party. This allowed him to justify his practice as a defense attorney and believe in fairness when it came to Law. I always noticed how guarded some statements and perspectives were. Especially, when it came to politics. It was clear the four of us who sat at this table were clearly from different places and at different stages in our lives, but we were all working towards one goal – my acquittal.

Our first days of court were spent jockeying and pontificating. The government, as always, came in well prepared or at least with the perception of being prepared. Perception would be everything at this point. This was the opening of a masterful chess game that put my life on the *board*. The Government had made its move. Now that we were in court, my team and I were now challenged to make the next move.

The chess game that was my life would be judged by federal court Judge John T. Regan. During my five years in Nashville, I had never heard of Judge Regan nor knew any agents that had been in his courtroom. I did my research and found he was appointed by President Jimmy Carter. He had been on the bench for 30 years and had the reputation of thinking himself to be equal with God. His hair was snow white and he wore a string bowtie with black rimmed glasses. He was literally *Colonel Sanders* in a black robe.

After being seated, Judge Regan humored himself and the courtroom as he called the room to order. Judge Regan was slow to speak, but it was obvious he was eager to move things along. Judge Regan longstanding appointment caused him to preside over the procedural stages and rules of engagement with a callous disregard. I felt like I was in a streetball basketball game, where there would be no fouls called unless blood was shed.

The first day began with considering potential jurors. This would be a strategic aspect of my case. It was critical to find 12 people who would pay attention to the technical aspects of wire fraud and the detailed elements of the crime I was accused of committing. There would be no murder plots, drug deals that went bad, or hush money paid with video cameras watching. It was a paper case. Just stacks of paper, but each sheet of paper meant something and could not be overlooked. It would take special jurors, ones that were used to paying attention to details.

At first, it did not dawn on me that there were only two African Americans in the pool. Nonetheless, within the first hour, they had been dismissed by the prosecution. I was not sure what this meant, but by the end of the next day, I had my jury who were not my peers. Unfortunately for me, I was in Nashville, Tennessee with an all-white jury who held my fate in their hands. The obvious was expressed by my attorney, but minimized to be insignificant by Judge Regan. As I looked back, I realize that Judge Regan had every intention of connecting with them and using his Southern charm to show them the facts of my case.

The United States' attorney representing the government went first. He was from Knoxville, Tennessee, and he was the second chair. As he began, I thought to myself, it was a little odd for him to make the opening statement, instead of the lead attorney. I remember his opening statement like it was yesterday. He began by telling a story about how he would go to a buffet restaurant as a child and fill his plate because it was all you could eat. He would take all this food back to his table and make every attempt to consume it, but quickly realized that his eyes were bigger than his stomach. He said I was the same guy he was at 8. The only difference is that I should have known better. He described me as someone possessed by greed, who bought houses I could not pay for and did it with dirty money. According to him, I loaded my plate with houses and when I could not pay for them, I decided to file bankruptcy.

Although his statements appeared true, I was certain everything he said would be clarified with a fiery rebuttal from Adam, my attorney, who I now considered a friend. However, I heard the rebuttal, but it was absent of any fire. Instead, in a soft tone, Adam presented what could be considered more of an excuse as opposed to an explanation. While Adam left the jurors wanting to hear more, his presentation of the facts lacked luster. Even though I was troubled about how my case began, Adam reassured me that it was a good day and cautioned me against wearing fancy suits to court. He reminded me that I had earned more and lost more than most of the jurors would in their lifetime.

When the government began day two, surprisingly, they announced this would be the final day of presenting the case against me. Wait! What happened to their string of witnesses and the mountain of evidence they were scheduled to present? My team and I were puzzled by this sudden turn of events. However, we had no choice, but to watch and wait.

The prosecution finally let the Pitbull off the porch. Sam Fist stood 6' 3" tall and commanded the attention and respect of everyone in the court, including the Judge. He put his witnesses on the stand and validated every one of their statements with overwhelming approval.

Adam took a stab at discrediting a couple of bank employees and the agent from the office of the inspector general, but he was not impactful. Seemingly, when Adam would make headway the Judge would shut him down through Fist's objections. I was becoming more and more concerned, but I was reassured that we would get our turn. While at the table, during the testimony, Adam wrote notes vigorously as if he had an ah huh moment. However, when his time came to cross examine, he became the *absent-minded professor*. Adam stood in a state of confusion, unsure if he should question the witnesses or get them off the stand, hoping the jury would quickly forget about them.

Even though my case was not going as well as planned, it was now our turn. The prosecution had rested its case and the defense would call its first witness. I had at least 3-5 witnesses that would easily give the true account of what had taken place. One of my most memorable witnesses was our handwriting expert. She was not just any kind of handwriting expert with a pocket square pen protector and a propeller hat. She was best described as a hip grandmother, a foxy senior, or a baby boomer that was on round three of a life filled with adventure.

She took the stand with her spiked grey hair and red leather jacket. She had the jurors' attention in her appearance alone. I had not seen her prior to her appearance in the courtroom, so I was just as shocked as the jurors. Her soft, confident Southern drawl didn't match her appearance, but right away, you could tell she knew what she knew, and she knew it well. She gave a detailed litany of her qualifications and 30 years of experience.

The big question was then asked. "Have you reviewed any of Mr. McAllister's handwriting samples?" "Yes, I have reviewed almost 20 years of his handwriting and I can tell you with 99% certainty this is not Mr. McAllister's handwriting." She was referring to a loan application that was completed that inflated my income. I had maintained from the beginning that I did not complete the loan application and never told anyone that I made $500,000.00 a year.

She was then asked again about her certainty and how she could make such an assessment. When she finished, it was clear to everyone that you better not question grandma. I finally felt some sense of relief. The air in the courtroom seemed to become lighter. I watched with optimism as a few jurors nodded their head in agreement. Adam turned it over to the prosecution and there was no attack, but a casual dismissal that this old lady possibly did not know what she was talking about and had been duped by me.

The entire pace and tenor of the room rapidly changed when it came to our mortgage expert, Gary. Gary was likeable and viewed as a credible jolly old soul. Gary was one of my few witnesses that I had gotten to know. He reviewed the documents in my case. Adam took an extensive amount of time allowing Gary to give his curriculum vitae credentials. The qualifications were extensive. He was not at all interesting and seemed to bore most of the jurors. Gary was an asset and displayed an unwavering support for me and what happened in my loan proceedings. However, Gary did not get off as easy as my handwriting expert. The prosecution immediately went on the attack and started discrediting Gary's qualifications as an expert.

They pitched him as a hired gun: the best money could buy. For the right amount of money, per the prosecution, he would say anything. This infuriated Gary, just as they had hoped. He took the bait and was no longer effective. Unfortunately for me, it was not a good day at the office.

Witnesses like Gary started to fall apart one by one. Some not remembering, others just too nervous to put two sentences together. Our last resort was calling Steve Samson, my loan officer. This was also a tense encounter. Thirty minutes prior to him walking in the courtroom to take the 5th, I had just walked around the corner to the elevators. I was in the process of putting my belt on from going through the metal detector. When I looked up, there he was. His 6'5" was insignificant to the rage that I felt coming up within me. He saw me and dashed into the elevator as if he could escape the thrashing he knew he deserved.

I stepped on the elevator and as much as I would like to say I was calm, cool and collected, the true saving grace was my attorney who was present, and the God that I was trusting to work on my behalf to bring the truth to the forefront. Getting off the elevator was like finally being able to breathe again after holding my breath under water. The elevator door could not open fast enough.

Just when I thought I could breathe, word came down that Steve was going to take the 5th. That was not a bad thing. It was actually in our favor and was a clear indicator that Steve did not want to say anything to incriminate himself. However, it would be the Judge's response that would cause a gut-wrenching blow to my case and cause Adam to lose his way. The Judge okayed the loan officer's plea.

The Judge's okay meant that Steve could take the 5th without the jurors knowing anything about it. He would not be mentioned to the jurors and the jurors would not even know he existed. They could not even consider Steve's actions because he was not mentioned in any context. This was the foundation of my defense. Steve had falsified my loan documents and based on the Judge's actions, he now did not exist. Checkmate!

Can't Get Out of Bed

There was nothing else to do, and no more witnesses to call, except myself. Could I save myself? Everyone knows the worst witness you can call is the defendant. The churning in my stomach and the dry mouth signaled all the classic signs of fight or flight. I could do neither. I had to stay and take it on the chin. I knew it was going to be bad when I started stuttering when asked my name by the defense. Two days later and I knew I did not hurt myself as bad as I could have, but I was not helpful either. It was over and now in the hands of the jurors.

The Judge was eager to take a break, not for the jurors, but because he had plans for Thanksgiving. He gave everyone a week off because he was traveling to the West Coast to visit his family. I needed the break and I was determined to be thankful. I enjoyed the meal with my family and watched a little football, but in the back of my mind, I was concerned about how I would be spending the next Thanksgiving. It was no certainty of what the outcome would be, but my faith and positive thinking would be the platform I would stand on to the end.

The week after Thanksgiving, I stood before a Judge and jury and heard the word, "Guilty!" I was numb. I had expected God to work on my behalf and reveal the truth. I had expected God to deliver me, but He did not. God had disappointed me because He did not do what I had expected. As I turned to walk out of the courtroom and saw the looks of failure in my attorney's eyes. I also saw my wife extending her arms to hug and comfort one of my other attorneys. "Shouldn't it be the other way around," I thought. My attorney should be comforting my wife.

Oddly with everything that was taking place, my mind went back to the juror who was wiping away tears as the Judge announced the verdict. I had noticed this woman because throughout the trial she was attentive to all the details. She had questioning looks when others seemed unconcerned and immediately accepted the words that were spoken by U.S. Attorney Fist. No one would question him, but she dared to shake her head *no* when he gave a subliminal nod of *yes* to information he knew was false or at least questionable.

This woman's bloodshot eyes were a clear indication that these tears were not new, but had been shed earlier and this verdict was not something she was comfortable accepting. It was obvious that this was not a slam dunk verdict because it took 2 1/2 days to reach. She was one of the few who looked back at me, but her look was not one of chastisement. It was a look of hope, belief, and compassion.

I felt her compassion and wished I could have spoken to her to say thank you for listening. Thank you for understanding how things happened. Thank you for taking this process seriously and recognizing that my life was on the line. I wanted to stand on the table and yell to the Judge and everyone present to ask her why she had been crying. What truth did she see in me? Unfortunately, I would not be able to do that. I had to accept the verdict for the moment. The Judge's final parting words were to be back in his courtroom in February. It was clear that he was not through with me yet.

The next week when families would normally be preparing for the Christmas holiday, I found myself in a fight for my life. I was mentally, emotionally, physically, and spiritually drained. There were days I did not want to get out of the bed, and other days, I just did not have enough strength to get out of bed. Many days I found myself in a fetal position with my mind racing and asking, "Why?" Despite the feelings of abandonment and betrayal, I forced myself to function with a sense of normalcy. But, what would be my new normal? What had been *normal* for the past 15 years was no longer a reality. I would soon get a glimpse of my new reality.

It was my daughter's birthday and I went to the store to pick up a birthday card. I found a card that I liked along with a pack of M&M's. I handed the cashier my debit card as I had routinely done for several years. I was surprised when I saw the word, "Declined." I gave it no thought and handed her another card. I was now embarrassed when it was also declined. I was looking at $4.22 declined. I gave the cashier an embarrassing nervous smile, "I'll be right back."

I went out to the car where I kept my spare change. I managed to come up with $1.72. I could not pay $4.22 to buy my daughter a birthday card. As I sat in the driver's seat of my car, my body began to shake uncontrollably. I quivered as tears began to pour like raindrops. I had made six figures, ran businesses that made millions, and managed millions of dollars in assets, and now I did not have $4.22 to buy my daughter a birthday card. I was a convicted failure of a man who thought he had nothing left.

When I looked up, I had been in a state of hopelessness for about an hour. I had to compose myself to make the 10-minute drive home. When I walked into our rented house, that I was uncertain of how much longer we could afford, Judy saw in my eyes that I was deeply troubled. Without me saying anything, she just embraced me. She held me and I felt the warmth of her hands touch my soul. I explained to her what had just occurred at the store. I was relieved that I could tell someone what I was feeling, but I hated that I was snatching the security blanket covering I had attempted to provide. The next thoughts were of me pushing a shopping cart and my family living from my car on the streets, but she spoke those words again. "Trust God! This is bigger than us." How could I trust God? He had just dealt me the greatest disappointment of my life. At this point, I was frustrated and did not want to hear those words.

Just when I thought things could not get any worse, I received one of the first calls from another agent in the FBI office

I was assigned to in Nashville. For the past six months, I was on administrative leave and technically still an employee of the FBI. Keith was a *matter-of-fact* type of supervisor that did have strong people skills, but even he couldn't make lemonade out of this lemon. Even so, I met him at a local restaurant, not knowing what to expect because I had previously been blindsided in our last encounter.

He was cordial and asked, "How are you doing? I can't imagine what you have been going through. There is no easy way to say or do this, but I was sent an immediate lead (an action notice that comes from FBI headquarters in D.C. that local FBI offices have no control over the content) to have you served with this letter of termination." I took a sigh and did not take it personally. It was clear Keith was just a messenger – a reluctant messenger at that. There was no way to soften this blow. The FBI was very procedural and there was no way they could have a convicted felon as an employee, so it was now officially over.

I took some time to read the official notice. The termination was clear. I was not allowed to divulge any information that would jeopardize any ongoing investigations. The language, although legal in nature, was clear to give notice that additional federal charges would be filed against me, and I would be prosecuted. I had seen it before and I knew it was not just an empty threat. After what I had just experienced, I had no intentions of challenging the system.

In less than 30 seconds, I reflected over my 15-year career and could not recall any formal complaints that had been filed against me. No disciplinary actions had been taken, or no procedural reprimands; my record was clean. During the trial and discovery, I could see where a background investigation had been conducted that went all the way back to my employment with the Los Angeles police department and there was nothing to even suggest less than an exemplary career in law enforcement. There were numerous awards and commendations that stood on their own merits. I had nothing to be ashamed of, except how it was ending.

I had to control my anger because I had no place to direct it. But, there was a rage inside me with the force of dynamite behind it. If I exploded, how many casualties would I cause and what would be the collateral damage? The anger shifted to disappointment that Keith did not understand. He was just carrying out the orders of the *executioner*. There was no more time to reflect. His nervous twitch indicated he was ready for this to be over with, and so was I.

I signed the forms and Keith looked away as if he was pulling the trigger on an old hunting dog he had to put out of its misery. It was clear, this *ole dog* would not hunt anymore. There would be no more early mornings to go get bad guys because they had been spotted in a local area. There would be no more high-fives because you talked the bad guy into confessing, and no all-nighters telling war stories to stay awake. It was over.

I slid the papers across the sticky wooden table. Keith offered to buy me a drink or something to eat. I took another sip of the sweet tea that had been placed in front of me. The strong smell of holiday cooking filled the air, but I had no appetite. "Thank you, man. I'm good."

His next words were off the record, "If I can do anything for you or your family, let me know." I thanked him and stood up to leave. He extended his hand as a kind gesture. "You take care," were his parting words.

The Christmas holidays are supposed to be a time of celebration, but I was struggling. I did not feel as if there was much to celebrate. We had a lean Christmas that year, and I explained to our children why. They accepted it, and we still celebrated as a family. This year's gifts were just going to be the hopes of putting a meal on the table. At least, that is what I thought.

After leaving Keith, I went to the post office and to my surprise, there was a Christmas card from a friend. But, the greater surprise was the $250.00 check that fell out. I believe it was God's little way of telling me that he was going to still take care of me. While I was sitting, being thankful, I got a call from Jerry, who was the leader of the men's Bible study I attended. He asked me to meet him at the bowling alley with my son in an hour.

Before I could say I did not have any money, he said, "Me and some of the brothers want to treat you and your boy. It will be father and son time." I graciously accepted his invitation, even though I did not feel like bowling. Maybe it would be a good outing for my son to hang out with Jerry's son who was a teammate.

While I was driving to pick up my son, Mike, the phone rang again and this time it was my pastor in Nashville. He invited my wife and I to have lunch with him and two other pastors the next day. Again, I was not interested, but accepted because I thought it would be good for Judy to get out and go someplace I knew I could not afford to take her. I picked up my son and handed Judy the check that came in the mail. I felt proud to be able to make some kind of a contribution, since I had not made any in several months.

Mike saw his buddies and then put on his game face. We are both innately competitive and we had father and son teams. Mike was not an experienced bowler, but I quickly discovered the other boys were not skilled either. It was the epidemic of too much PlayStation and electronic games. Even so, the competitive nature that exists in every male species came out. We won and it was fun. Gone was the pity party and despondency I had felt earlier in the day. I knew I would have to face the reality of the day, but not before I was given a shopping bag.

Jerry, took me to his car and asked how everything was going. He had been in the courtroom with me on several occasions. He was a warm and compassionate guy that took a sincere interest without hesitation. He spoke simple words, as he handed me the bag, "Me and the guys want you to know that we love you. It's not much and we wish we could do more, but we hope this helps." There was no additional dialogue, just a massive embrace and a firm pat on the back. I was encouraged and believed I could make it.

The shopping bag was generic and unassuming. When I got home, I was sitting with Judy and began pulling out wrapping paper. The wrapping paper was nice and I figured Judy would divide up the $250.00 check and purchase gifts for the kids to wrap up. Then I began opening the cards. With every card I opened, out fell a gift card, another gift card, another Visa card, another American Express card. I finally got it. The gift cards were to go out and buy our gifts and the paper was to wrap them up. The love of my friends and family was overwhelming. On what I thought was one of the worst days of my life since hearing *guilty*, my hope was renewed with the outpouring of love.

It always amazes me how God has a way of restoring hope when it seems like it has been snatched away. If people try to snatch your joy, God uses others to come running in your direction to restore it. That is exactly what I experienced. I had always heard the words that God uses people, and I knew it to be true. But, now I had experienced it firsthand. It was no longer just someone else's experience; this was my story — my life.

My first ray of hope came when I was told that my sentencing date would be postponed because of another trial. I made up in my mind that I was not going to sit and have a pity party while I waited for my sentencing date. Shortly after that, on the third day of January, I received a call that the pastor of the small church we were attending was sick. I was asked to come and help run the revival. I accepted because I probably needed reviving more than anyone. The preacher came and shared powerful words every night and I just listened and believed God that the new year was going to bring a great turn around.

Well, the turnaround started with the pastor of the church. He was sicker than anyone realized and when he came to church, we had to pray for him. I, unexpectedly, had to preach. I preached the best I could and prayed my best prayers believing God for his healing. I must admit, I was surprised at how quickly the pastor recovered. He shared his testimony and patted me on the back saying, "Carry on son," as he went to check on another church. He was the Bishop and had to oversee the work of over 50 churches and he was now trusting me to care for one of the churches under his jurisdiction. Everything seemed to turn in my favor.

I reviewed the transcripts of my case and began looking for another attorney. I was still broke, but was convinced that a good attorney could reverse this outcome and get me restored in some way. The fees for an appeal were high and there were not many interested in cleaning up someone else's work. I found an old hunter that spoke the local language. We clicked right away. He showed me a book of pictures that captured some of his big kills in Canada and Wyoming. He then told me, "There are others that are cheaper, but not better. I can get someone to do the legwork for you and that will save you a little." I signed on the bottom line with the hope and prayer I could raise his $10,000.00 retainer.

I was notified again that the new sentencing date was going to change because it was set for "Good Friday" by accident. So, I was now looking at some time in June. It would soon be a whole year since this terrible nightmare had started. I had no idea what it would all entail, but what I was amazed by is that I had survived. I survived the unthinkable and the unimaginable and was waiting to see the fullness of my miracle.

At the church, I was preaching and teaching trust and faith in God on every occasion. These were the messages I needed to hear and came from my heart. The congregation seemed to enjoy them and came out faithfully. I caught myself because there had never been any formal announcement or discussion of my conviction or what I was facing. I was not sure if anyone knew or if anyone cared. So, on one Sunday I did the unthinkable, and put it all out there. I needed their prayers and what I was facing with the sentencing coming up in several weeks. They all responded with overwhelming kindness and loved on my wife and children.

Shortly after the 4th of July, I walked back into the courtroom I had not seen in six months. This time I was equipped with two attorneys, my former and my new one. I felt like I had a cloud of witnesses supporting me—six friends that would be personal character witnesses and over 30 letters that had been sent to the judge in advance. Within minutes, it was clear the Judge was not interested in hearing anything anyone had to say. He wanted to get it over with and move on to his afternoon activities.

He slightly entertained the first gentlemen who spoke, Eddie White. Eddie had known me a shorter period and represented the seasoned wisdom that knew good men when he saw them. Eddie was simple in his speech and direct. His snow-white hair did not just reflect his wisdom, but the perspective that he spoke from went against everything I was made out to be during the trial. Eddie spoke with such conviction and confidence that he made you listen. Next to the Judge, he was the most senior person in the courtroom. He and the Judge could have easily traded places.

The next person to speak was a young lady that Judy and I adopted into our family. We were extremely proud of her because she had just graduated from Vanderbilt University. She affectionately called me "Pops." She shared from her heart what I meant to her and the guidance I had given. It brought me to tears to hear someone share their true feelings about me. Her words were kind and warm until she started to shed her tears. The Judge did not want to see that in his courtroom, so he dismissed her.

We saved my best friend for last. He had known me and my character better than anyone in the courtroom. We had 20 years of adventures together. There were not too many days that went by that we did not talk at least once. He decided to be a storyteller and drop names of highly respected individuals that trusted me. The Judge was not impressed and his expressions showed it.

Adam, my former attorney, was asked if I wanted to say anything and my new attorney had strongly advised me not to say anything. I waived my right to speak on my own behalf. It was if the Judge was finally pleased with one thing that took place that morning. He wasted no time and imposed a sentence of 48 months, 36 months' probation, and $700,000 in restitution. Just before he concluded, my new attorney spoke up and advised he would be representing me and made a Fist request that I be given 60 days to report to prison. For the first time, the Judge granted my request.

I was still in a semi-state of shock. It was the time that I expected to experience some of the favor I believed God was supposed to grant me. I was told that the Judge could have given me a sentence that was as simple as probation and community service. I was obviously no threat to the community. The outrageous guidelines allowed the Judge to sentence me to as much as 72 months. The translation is six years in a federal prison for a non-violent, non-drug related crime that I did not commit. He took the middle ground to make a statement.

It was clear to everyone in the courtroom that the Judge took none of what was said or written to him into consideration. He did not take any time to deliberate. His mind had been made up before the proceeding. We had just gone through the motions as a formality. As I stood to walk out, I saw the glassy eyes and tears of my friends and family that had been quickly wiped away. I got some gentle pats on the back and some comforting words of confidence, but the blow was still stinging. My last resort would be my appeal.

I had 30 days to get my appeal written and filed with the Appellate Court. The 6th Circuit was tough, but my new attorney was confident he could present a convincing argument to get an emergency hearing and a stay which would delay me having to report to begin serving my sentence. Brian was short in stature, but gigantic in his aggressive approach in presenting the arguments of my appeal. The central argument would be based on the constitutional right of being tried by a jury of your peers. I did not have a jury of my peers. There were no African Americans on my jury. It was hard to believe, but it was a fact that an all-white jury in Tennessee had convicted me for a crime I did not commit.

I had read history books and heard stories about the dangers of an all-white jury and a black defendant in the south, but I was now living it. This would be the basis of my appeal. You could tell he understood and was prepared to strongly argue this injustice. I bought into his argument and believed this was the best approach, even though there were numerous areas in the trial that were procedurally inappropriate and borderline unethical.

Sixty days later, after finishing a Bible study, I told those in attendance that this might be my last Bible study for a while. The time had come for me to finally report to a prison camp by the end of the week. The saints began to pray, and speak words of encouragement that God would work everything out and we would meet next week at the same time and same place. Two days later, I was driving myself to prison to turn myself in.

The only experience that compared to this were the days when mama would send me outside to get my own switch. I humored myself with these thoughts on the 3 1/2-hour drive. Judy was by my side in the car. My concern was about who was going to take care of my family while I was gone. I believed that my new attorney would have my appeal heard and have me home within 30 days.

After six weeks, he broke the news to me that it would be at least 12 months before my appeal would be heard. My disappointment and frustration had now turned into anger and bitterness. I was done crying out to God. I was just shaking my head asking, "Why?" I was now in a prison surrounded by many men that felt the same way I did. Many were cursing God and wanted to hear nothing about Him.

One day as I was passing the chapel, I heard the words in my spirit, "What are you willing to sacrifice to change the way another man spends eternity?" I paused for that moment and heard them again, "What are you willing to sacrifice to change the way another man spends eternity?" My heart that had begun to harden started changing in that moment. The 36 months that I would spend in prison was nothing compared to eternity. Christ gave the perfect example of sacrifice and changed the way we all can spend eternity.

Chicken Day

Little did I realize every day would be a fight to survive. I was sacrificing three years of my life. Part of me was dying while another part was struggling to make sense of it all, so I could somehow survive. I had heard it said, but I was now experiencing the belief that being in prison is the closest you can come to death while still being alive. It was as if I was trapped in a never-ending nightmare. The challenge of getting past the initial shock of staying up all night staring at the locker in front of me was starting to fade. I spent my nights with my back against the cold painted cinder block wall because I did not know what happened at night in the open dorms. None of the cubes had doors. It was open space with five-feet high cinder block walls dividing each portion of *real estate*.

Upon my arrival, my *celli* as they were called, did not have much to say because I was invading his space. He introduced himself as "Dry." "How appropriate," I thought. He never said which bunk was mine; it was just understood I had the top bunk. The tough part was there being no ladder and either you used a chair or if you were athletic and in good shape, you jumped and pushed yourself up on the five-feet high bed. I was not good at getting to the top bunk, and the fear of falling and embarrassing myself loomed over me like a dark cloud. By the third night, I tried to sleep in my assigned place, and finally I was given instruction on how to climb on the top bunk without killing myself.

The men that were around me were not as mean as I had expected. However, they were not kind, gentle, soft spoken, or polite either. It was simply about respect. If I minded my own business and did not disrespect anyone else, I would be fine. The controlled terror I had been feeling was starting to subside, but I still had my guard up. Ultimately, the stress of the initial entry was taking a toll on me physically.

I had a constant headache and barely ate any of the food. However, my stomach would growl and nothing out of an institutional beige tray looked appealing. I missed my wife, Judy, and my children. I was ready to go home. If this was supposed to be my punishment, I had my share and I would be good for the rest of my life. "Please, somebody let me go home," was my daily thought. My feelings were insignificant in a place where 500 out of 500 men felt the same way. So, there was no sympathy or condolences from anyone. I had to suck it up, toughen up, and shut up because no one wanted to hear a whiner that thought they should not be in prison.

A callus state of mind was starting to consume me. For most of my life I had been considered a compassionate person. When I saw a need or someone in trouble, I tried to help. If nothing else, I tried to listen. But now, I did not even want to listen. Now I had blinders on and did not see the pain and frustration on the faces of those around me. I felt myself hardening. I would hear the complaints, pain, anger, frustration, and bitterness, but now they were just sound waves that were now bouncing off my hardened heart.

As I was settling into this toxic mindset, a group of Christian brothers invited me to the chapel to meet the "brothers" on the compound. I was hesitant because I was certain there was not much these guys could tell me about being a Christian, and I most certainly was not on the lookout for jail house religion. I did not need anything else adding to my frustration. It was game night at the chapel, and *Bible Jeopardy* was the highlight of the night. I was impressed with something I had not seen in the week I had been there. I was given a can of soda and a bag filled with chips. Initially, I was hesitant to accept it because nothing in prison is free, but this was free. For the first time, I witnessed real kindness, men laughing, and having genuine fun. I was the new guy, so I was thrown on one of the four teams that competed for prizes at the end.

Instantly, my competitive nature came out. I have been competitive all my life and quickly realized that every man in the room had the same drive to win as me. In the short time I had been at the prison, I noticed this was a classic characteristic of 95% of the men; they had a drive to win. It made no difference if it was softball, basketball, pool, shuffleboard, cards, dominos, weightlifting, or just a foot race, each of us had the same drive to win.

Now, I had a chance to shine with what I knew about the Bible. On the first question asked, I gave the answer. "Correct!" I answered the next one too. "Correct, again!" Now, I was getting a little attention. A tougher question was asked, and I answered without hesitation. "Correct!" "Who's the new guy?" The facilitator was intrigued by someone who could answer his questions. The next question I answered with bold confidence. "Wrong!" Everyone began to laugh in great amusement.

"Wait!" I protested. Even though my answer was partially correct, it was not the answer the judge wanted. Little did I know; the game was fixed and the judge was never wrong. It was explained to me that it was not so much about winning, but to have a little fun in prison and show Christian love.

As time went by, I discovered that I did not know as much as I thought. There were men there that were former gang members, major drug dealers, cons, thieves, and master manipulators. They had now made a change or were seeking to make greater changes. They studied their Bibles intensely and had a good understanding, but still had questions. I learned from that night that I did not need to show how much I knew, but how much I was willing to learn from men that most would not expect to learn anything.

Very few guys went by their true name. Prison was much like the streets where everyone used monikers. Having a street name made it more difficult to be identified and a person's street name carried a certain level of credibility and reputation. I heard names like "Black, Boo, Bear, Bamma, Monster, Smoke, Rev, Sky, Outlaw, New York, Do Boy, Man, City," or just initials that did not represent the individual's real name.

My first job was in the garage. I knew absolutely nothing about cars, besides driving and putting gas in them. I made friends with a guy from Nashville who worked in the kitchen. He explained that I could work in the kitchen and experience some of the benefits from being in prison. I had no idea what he was talking about until I spent my first full week in the kitchen.

The kitchen was run like a dope house with food being the primary commodity. There were kingpins, runners, sellers, and plenty of buyers. You did not make much in the kitchen, but you made up for it by hustling the food. I started at 25 cents an hour. You could buy everything from an onion to a carton of milk. Items high in protein like eggs, chicken, and peanut butter were always high on the demand list. The biggest day was Thursday because it was chicken day. Chicken was provided in leg quarters. Every inmate got a quarter of a leg for lunch. It might be fried, baked, or barbecued. Kitchen workers got the leftovers. The amazing thing was few leftovers were ever seen by the guards. However, leftovers were to be eaten in the kitchen, by the kitchen staff. Unfortunately, this never happened.

I watched and learned quickly that there were guys making a lot of money off chicken, eggs, and the most precious of them all, sugar. Sugar was in a class all by itself. Like dope on the streets, it was the crack cocaine of the prison. Sugar could be used to make hooch which was prison wine made from fruit. This powerful concoction was one step below moonshine. The food was sold just like dope, with a distribution network that was untraceable. Postage stamps were the trading commodity. U.S. currency of any kind was unnecessary on the premises because there was nothing you could buy with it. All your funds were put on your electronic account and maintained by computer. But, stamps were used to gamble, buy food, and trade for services. A stamp was worth about 40 cents. Three stamps cost a dollar. A quarter of a leg went for three stamps. You quickly knew who the ballers were or those individuals who had money to spare. Their food was delivered on time, hot from the kitchen by runners. They paid with stamps and had regular accounts set up which they settled weekly through purchases from the commissary.

The choice was how deeply entrenched would I become in this segment of prison life. There were already established rules of engagement. If they did not know you or trust you, they did not deal with you. But if they thought you had money on your books and came from a background that could pay; you got credit and plenty of it. You could get a *credit rating* of 800 plus. But, if you tried to back out on paying your bill, word traveled quickly and no one would deal with you.

At first, I was torn. I wanted to make money off what was being sold in the kitchen, but I was not a thief. I worked hard, and got food. So, I just decided to give it away. I quickly learned, that was a bad idea. Word got out and I was cut off. I was *bad for business*. I was devaluing a trade system that was part of the culture.

One of the guys, by the name of "Spanky," pulled me aside and explained things to me. "You can't give the food away. It's yours. Sell it or eat it, but don't go around giving it away. Make yourself a little money and play the game." I felt uneasy and anxious. I was not one that disregarded the rules. For most involved in the food trade, there was not a second thought or remorse. I could not become someone or something that I was not. There were many guys to remind you no matter what you decided to do, you were no better than them. You were a criminal, a convict, and an inmate because you were in the same place with them. I was torn and had to make a choice.

I was respected for being involved in the church, but I would be a hypocrite if I stole from the kitchen and sold the food back to the men. I rationalized and justified the fact that the food belonged to the men. I would only accept what was given out to me and give it away to the men I knew did not have much. I made my room a place where men that had no one on the outside sending them anything could get a little extra to eat. They had to promise they would not tell anyone I had given it to them. That was not hard for them to do because they did not want to get cut off either.

I decided that sacrificing my integrity and character was not an option. I was going to stand my ground and not give in to the temptation to *go along to get along*. My time in the kitchen was short-lived and rapidly came to an end. Little did I know, my stand would attract even more attention, but my survival in prison was just beginning.

On December 23rd, my name was called over the loud speaker. "McAllister, report to Administration Building." This meant one of two things: you had to give a urine sample or you possibly might be getting an early release. I was hoping and praying for the latter. I marched myself a quarter mile across the compound with a bitter cold wind blowing in my face. Each turn intensified my anxiety on the news waiting for me. In the last hundred yards, I was convinced I would have to give a urine sample since I had been there almost three months and had not given one yet. I stepped out of the cold onto the high glossed waxed floors. These floors were the signature welcoming mat that visitors saw when they came to see their relatives. They left an impression in their mind that this place was spotless and immaculately clean.

I knocked on the wood framed door with the tinted window that prevented you from seeing inside. I felt like I had been called to the principal's office and had no idea what I had done, but knew I was in trouble. "Come in! Who is it?" was the Southern drawl response.

"McAllister."

"Who called you?"

Before I could respond, a voice from another room responded, "I did." I walked through the common area to the corner office with windows. It was Ms. Smith, my counselor. I had only seen her one time in the three months I had been at the prison. "Close the door, and have a seat." As I sat down, she handed me a certified letter, and a clipboard with a pen attached. "You have to go to court, and they will pick you up next week. Merry Christmas."

The return address was from the U.S. Marshal and the contents of the letter were short and to the point. I was being summoned by the defense to testify in a case I had worked as an agent. Well, there went my hopes of an early release. Then, after Ms. Smith's explanation of what my transport would consist of, I would have much preferred taking the urinalysis. "You are going to be transported to Baton Rouge by the U.S. Marshal. They will pick you up next week sometime and get you there. One of the guards will get a bag to you, so you can pack up all of your stuff." Her words were very matter-of-fact, which left me with more questions than the answers.

"What if I don't want to go and testify?"

"You don't have a choice and you need to work that out with your attorney. Sign here and we will talk later." I was trying to slow her down, but I could tell this was an interruption in her daily flow.

"Will I be transported by myself or with others? Do they drive me the whole way?" She smiled with a face that had been over made up with Christmas colored make-up. Now I knew why they called her *Lady Gaga*.

"You self-surrendered, didn't you? Have you ever been held in custody?"

"I..."

"This may be a little rough on you, but you will be okay." Her commentary was not helping at all. She pointed to the clipboard, "Sign right there." She was now rushed as she waived me to the door. "Call your attorney if you have questions."

I was in the shiny hallway within five seconds wondering, "What just happened?"

The quarter-mile walk back to my dorm seemed to have gotten longer and filled with more questions than I had going. As soon as I got in my cube, I pulled out my telephone book and marched over to the phone to call my attorney. It was the Thursday afternoon before Christmas weekend and he was not in the office. I had a special contact number, so I called him on his cell phone. Although the extra 100 minutes to talk on the phone was for Christmas calls, I was willing to use all my minutes to get my questions answered by my attorney.

Again, no answer. The next best thing was to send him an email. I braved the cold elements that seemed to have gotten colder. I walked in the computer room and inmates were pecking away with the two-finger shuffle trying to type as fast as they could in the 30 minutes they were allowed to be on the computer. It was almost comical, but I did not have time to appreciate it because there was one computer open, and I had to get to it before it was taken. I joined the pecking chorus and sent my attorney a quick note explaining what had just happened and the fact I had no desire to travel to Baton Rouge to testify in anyone's court.

Plan B, most times, works better than the original. You could always get information in prison because inmates were valued by what they knew. The same rule applied on the streets. If you knew the right people, places, or things, you were an asset. I was a trained investigator, and I was on a mission to work for my best client, me. I strolled into the gym where the Christmas basketball tournament was in full effect. The plan was to pull a couple of the best sources aside and give them hypotheticals such as, "Do you know anyone that has gone back to court? What's transport like? Do you know anyone that has gotten out of going to court?" Immediately, a flood of resources started coming in. Unfortunately, all the reports were contradicting one another. I was not making much progress, but I was determined to get answers.

The next day, while I was in the kitchen, I tapped *Spanky* as my next source. He had a way of making folks believe just about anything: real, true, or imagined. Once you got through the imagined part, you could run with about 20 percent of what he told you. What do you know? *Spanky* pointed me in the direction of a new guy that just came on the compound. He had come from court and was transferred to our facility. He seemed quiet and I did not know him, but I watched him for a couple of days before I talked to him.

The set up could not be more perfect. I saw him playing shuffle board in the gym and this was my time to strike. I was the shuffle board king and knew I could beat him even though he had just won, giving me the opportunity to play him. The goal was not to beat him; it was to challenge him. I started off winning 7 – 1, then 10 – 7, we tied at 18 - 18, he won 19 – 21. "Great game" was my salute. I watched him play one of my partners that I regularly beat. He lost miserably 21 - 7. I consoled him and began to work him. Within 10 minutes, he was telling me everything I needed to know about going to court. Some of the information I had heard before and misinformation was dismissed. I was proud of myself for getting the information. However, I felt even more terrible because being in transport through the U.S. Marshal was not the ticket. My only hope was to contact my attorney and get a furlough. Little did I know, I would be laughed at with total disbelief that I was even asking for something so ridiculous as a furlough. The next morning, I had an email response from my attorney. He instructed me to call him on Tuesday the 26th of December, the day after Christmas. It was difficult to enjoy my first Christmas in prison with the transport hanging over my head.

Spending Christmas in prison had to be one of my lowest moments since being in prison. I experienced a heaviness and depression that brought such a feeling of hopelessness. Instead of getting gifts, I received a bag of snacks and candy to help me make it through the long weekend. I saw guys reading and rereading their Christmas cards. I saw others seemingly go into a coma and just sleep the weekend away. They just slept for about 48 hours. Others refused to acknowledge that Christmas existed. They never broke stride and just stuck to their normal routine.

My Christmas day meal was nice with all the trimmings. Just like other meals, this specialty was no different, with extras being sold to the highest bidders. It was re-prepared with a twist. Some of the Hispanic inmates made tacos and Spanish rice. Some of the black inmates made sweet potato turnovers, a nice spin on sweet potato pies. There was no limit on creativity. Makeshift coolers were made to keep the food from going bad. Microwaves were used to reheat the feast and keep the festivities going.

Despite how I was feeling, and with everything going on around me, I focused my energies on thinking about the task at hand, my furlough. Tuesday morning, I got to a phone and placed the call to my attorney. I had saved half of my extra 100 minutes for holiday calls to speak with my attorney, and on my first call, there was no answer. Frustration was growing in me like a soda bottle that had been shaken. My prayer was that no one would try to pop my top. I called again and there was no answer. Then I heard, "McAllister, report to the C.O. office."

"What now," was my internal response. I could not call again because I had no idea about what I did this time. There were four other names called with mine and I was the second one to get there.

"Let me know when everyone gets here. I'm only saying this once." Thankfully, as he finished his statement, the fourth inmate showed up. "Take these bags and put your stuff in them." You are going to be picked up in the next couple of days. "Get everything together." We were handed army green canvas duffle bags; again, I walked away with more questions than answers.

When I returned to my cube, the questions started bombarding me. "Where are you going? Where are they shipping you? Are you sick? What's up?" Whether I liked it or not, I was under the microscope. It was not just me, but everyone watched each other to make sure the other was not getting something that they should not or if they had discovered a new way to work the system. I was viewed as a *smart guy* that may have figured out a new scheme. Little did they know; I was just as confused as I was the first day I showed up. I was on the edge and it would not take much to push me over.

I regrouped and went back to making phone calls to my attorney. I got him, he was ready to make pleasantries and ask about the holidays. This was not that kind of call. I had to get right to the point because I only had 15 minutes. Out of all the questions I asked, he had no answers. But, he would check and get back to me. I told him how important it was to get this done, but also how important it was for me to schedule a time to speak with him again.

There was a loophole that I could use to call him back. Inmates were entitled to legal calls through their counselor, and it would not take away from the allotted monthly time. The next day I went to my counselor and requested a legal call. She was not in, and there were no other counselors available. Again, I found myself frustrated and ready to explode. Inmates always talked about how lazy and unhelpful the counselors are on good days. For them, there was no urgency, and they could care less about what I needed. I was told by a secretary to come back tomorrow, and my counselor should be able to help me. I walked out of the office feeling dejected because my plan was not coming together. There was nothing I could do to take my mind off making the phone call to my attorney. So, I took the time to write out every one of my questions. I was now organized and well equipped to work my plan of getting a furlough.

It was 10:00 a.m. the next morning, when I walked into the Administrative Building. Ms. Smith was there and she seemed to still be in a festive mood from the holidays. She was wearing one of those Christmas sweaters that had to come from someone she loved because it was the ugliest sweater I had ever seen. She greeted me with, "Well, what can I do for you, Mr. McAllister?"

"I would like to call my attorney."

"You would? Well, I'm not sure if we are calling attorneys today."

Little did I know, she was trying to be humorous, so I quickly interjected, "I have a scheduled appointment with him."

"Is this regarding your subpoena?"

"Yes, he is working on a furlough for me." All Ms. Smith's kindness immediately disappeared. She looked at me over her diamond studded readers, with her head cocked to the side and her spiked tinted hair.

"You're not getting a furlough from here, not unless the court orders you one," was stated in a stern commanding voice.

I fought back "Well, that's what my attorney is working on."

"What's the number?" She dialed it and handed me the receiver.

The call was brief, and my attorney had made no more progress and had no additional information than when I spoke with him several days earlier. My counselor was right. The court would need to order the furlough. "The court won't order you a furlough because you are in the custody of the Bureau of Prisons and it would take too long to get you on a calendar before you are transported."

"Okay! Well, let me know if anything changes, and if you can do anything." Wanting to scream, I handed Ms. Smith the phone. She hung it up. "How are they going to transport me as an FBI agent with a bunch of other guys, and where will they keep me?"

"You'll be okay." Her words were not very comforting.

New Year's Day had come and there was no more talk about me going anywhere. Everyone was watching the football games and more focused on celebrating a new year. All I could think about was I was getting one step closer to going home. Another year down.

A faithful tradition had been broken for me. For the past 25 years, I brought the New Year in at church, praying, and giving thanks for the blessing of another new year. I was now in prison far from anything familiar, but I still decided I would get with some other Christian brothers I had met and pray the New Year in regardless of where I found myself.

The Fight to Survive

The new year brought much more than I expected. If only I could have somehow foreseen the future, I would have found a time machine to keep me in the old year. My 25-year-old tradition of starting the year on my knees in a physical church was broken. I held hands with other men in a circle and prayed. Regardless of my environment, it was the sincerest and most powerful New Year's Eve prayer I had ever prayed over the last 25 years. I considered this to be a fact because it was the worst storm of my life.

Two days later, I heard my name called over the loud speaker to come to the Administration Building. I had not heard from my attorney and I had not spoken with my counselor. The option of a furlough had not even been considered, so there I stood with four other men ready for transport. Before I knew it, I was piled up in a pickup truck with a green duffle bag, I had packed five days earlier, with two men I knew and two I had only seen a few times. Two at a time, we squeezed into the little white truck to take the half mile ride to the medium security prison.

The medium security prison was where much more violent and serious prisoners are housed. This was the first time I had seen this area of the prison since I self-surrendered in September. Gone was the green grass. Now there was a quarter inch dusting of fresh snow that blew across the brown Kentucky grass. My hand cracked from the cold when I grabbed my bag out of the back. Everything I owned and had accumulated in the last three months was in my 50-pound bag.

My bag was inventoried by the guard as soon as I arrived. There was a long check sheet that itemized every item. The guard commented on how many books I had. "I normally don't take these many books. You must be a preacher or something. They are all religious, huh?" He responded in his *hillbilly* accent. He continued after taking a spit from his tobacco. "Well, maybe you might help some of these *fellars*." I nodded my head as if to agree.

I was disgusted by his lack of professionalism, but I guess he did not feel obligated to impress anyone. We were lined up and given the strip search instructions. This was so dehumanizing, but this was nothing compared to what I would experience next. Up to this point, I had never been physically behind bars, handcuffed, or held in an excessively restrictive manner. A light blue pair of paper pants, and a smock shirt were thrown at me. "Put these on and line up! Let's get moving. That bus will be here in 10 minutes."

The pants were excessively big, but I did not dare ask for a smaller size. I knew not to attract any unnecessary attention. I would soon discover that I should have said something. I was waiting for additional clothing, but nothing came but a flat pair of canvas shoes. I squeezed into them but they were too small. "Hey!

Get up here on this box!" I turned to see what I never imagined. A three feet high wooden box that was worn and scuffed with the past presence of countless men standing as if being placed on auction blocks to be sold into slavery.

Inmates were told to stand on this box as I heard heavy metal chains clanging. There were about eight sets that just kept reverberating. I flinched, as the chains rattled, feeling like the grim reaper's next victim. I felt the fight or flight adrenaline rising in me. I did not want chains placed on me. I was not going anywhere. Plus, I was complying with every request. Before I knew it, words were coming out of my mouth, "Do you have to put those on me?" I had spoken my thoughts without a filter. An immediate hush fell over the entire processing area. It was as if I had just challenged God to a fist fight.

Two guards took up defensive positions as the guard with the chains looked at me as if he was going to wrap the chains around my neck. "Did you say something?" as he stared me down.

I did not back down, "I'm not going anywhere and my counselor said it was up to you if I would be handcuffed."

He fired back, "Well, she told you right. It is up to me, and I'm getting ready to put these here chains on you."

Before I could respond again, two heavy metal shackles were slapped around my ankles with an eighteen-inch chain connecting them. I looked down to feel the coldness of the metal coming through my thin cotton socks. Another chain was slung around my waste, squeezed tight, and connected to the chains on my ankles. Handcuffs were put on me with my hands in front and then attached to the chain at my waste. Once the handcuffs were on, the other guards went back to doing their paper work.

I was treated just like any other inmate being transported, except for one of the brothers I knew from the chapel. He had been down for over 20 years and was being moved to a medical facility. He had been made the trustee and was responsible for loading the food and water. I guess they figured he was less of a threat than I was at the time. I tried not to let the fact that he was one of three white guys that was being transported bother me. Everyone else was black or Hispanic.

"Let's get going. We are running late!" A guard yelled across the processing area. Lined up two by two, the 12 of us were on our way out. I heard the buzz. The door with a one-inch bolt lock popped and the heavy metal door open. "Stay together!"

The bitter cold wind whipped around the corners of the metal door like a wolf looking for its prey. It bit right through the paper-thin pants I was wearing and went straight to my bones. I dropped my head as I started plowing through. It had started snowing again and another ½ inch was on the ground. I felt the icy ground coming through the bottom of my thin canvas shoes.

I wanted to run the 200-yards to the bus, but I would have been shot on the spot as a potential escapee. Even if I had been allowed to run, I could not. The chains prevented me from even walking fast. The chains only allowed me to take a 12-inch stride. I quickly learned that no one took a full stride because the ankle shackles cut into your skin. So, like everyone, I took a hop shuffle.

This was the same walk I had seen on "Roots" and other movies depicting slaves being moved onto slave ships in chains. The only chain missing was the one I had seen placed around their necks. My life had come to this? Every step I took was physically painful, but nothing compared to the humiliation I felt inwardly. I could not shed a tear. I could not complain. I had to take it like a man. I had to take it like so many other black men before me had taken it.

Instead of a slave ship, there was a generic coach bus that was the opposite of luxury. It had been retrofitted with grates on the windows and a steel cage that kept everyone five-feet behind the driver. The seats were hard plastic and built for those who were under five foot nine. At 6 foot, and 220 pounds, I had to go in sideways and scoot backwards.

A young man that had been picked up before our stop did not give anyone room to complain. At 6 foot 2 and 300 pounds he had gotten stuck in his seat and had to go to the bathroom. He was a comedian and made fun of himself and the whole transport. It was his way of coping, and it worked until he talked himself to sleep. In fact, we all fell into a deep sleep, until we were startled by what sounded like a gun shot.

The bus came to a screeching halt on the side of the highway. The four guards with shotguns in their hands started scrambling. I recognized they were going through emergency protocols. I did not see anyone trying to attack the bus, but I could not see the rear from my seat. Then I heard, "I knew we shouldn't have taken this piece of crap. They didn't fix nothing and just put us out here. They gonna pay my overtime too."

Five hours, and a cold cheese burger later, we were on our way to Atlanta. If I would have known what was waiting in Atlanta, I would have hoped for the bus to completely break down. As we arrived in Atlanta, I noticed all the familiar landmarks I had known going back and forth on Interstate 75. In all my travels, I never imagined I would picture Atlanta from this perspective. My legs had fallen asleep two hours earlier; they were now completely numb.

Atlanta intake, holding, and transport was an old United States penitentiary that had been closed 10 years earlier because of its deplorable conditions. It was re-opened as a temporary housing facility after 20 million dollars' worth of improvements, like running water and new toilets. Unfortunately, they both worked about 50 percent of the time.

In the black of the night at 2:00 a.m., the prison looked like an abandoned warehouse. Nothing looked as if it could live behind the 10-feet high cement walls. The bus finally came to a stop after going through three check points to a secure unloading area. The bus now smelled like a locker room of a defeated football team of grown men. I could not wait to get fresh air.

Somehow, I had forgotten the time and temperature sign I had seen on Interstate 75. However, I was quickly reminded it was 12 degrees.

The receiving guard made us stop because it was his smoke break. I did not think it could happen, but I watched one of the white guys who was with us turn blue as his body shook violently in the cold. The black men just cursed as the guard slowly took a drag from his cigarette. He was oblivious to it all.

Once we got inside, 60 degrees felt like a sauna. That was another complaint about the Atlanta correctional facility. It had no heat and no air conditioning. The processing guards had on hats and several layers of clothing. One guy made the mistake of asking for an extra blanket. "We already don't have enough to go around." There was no further discussion.

I was put in a temporary holding cell and immediately surrounded by complete darkness. All I heard were sounds around me as I held a blanket in what I thought might be the center of the cell. Again, I asked myself, "How did my life sink to such a low place?" As I walked, I realized my ankles were sore from the shackles, so I gingerly walked to the thin mat that covered the steel that was my bunk.

Lights turned on, locks buzzed, and metal doors popped opened. "Stand in front of your doors and don't come out until you are told, this is a head count and I.D. check!" The guard yelling looked like a drill sergeant from the marines. He was no non-sense and commanded respect. "Name! Number!"

"McAllister 1965-0075," He never made eye contact. I had been reduced to a body and a number. My only solace, was that I was leaving Atlanta the next day.

I was processed for transport out in the morning. I started hearing stories and realized how fortunate I was. One of the guys had challenged a guard on where he wanted to go and wrote a complaint. He was now going to one of the least desirable prisons in the system, somewhere in Louisiana. It was called *diesel therapy*. This is where you get transported around to the 5-10 locations, so you have no place to settle. Consequently, you cannot get visits because your family never knows where you are at any given time. It is an abusive form of discipline that is justified with a pen by administrators that see you as a *problem child*.

We were given leftover brown paper bags with molded bologna sandwiches and rotten fruit from an obviously travel-damaged plastic bin. When I opened the bag, the smell alone let me know mine was bad. Some men said they had religious diet restrictions, so they could get a fresher sandwich. It worked for some, but most just threw it away because they did not want to get sick in transport. One of the guys who was pretty built up from lifting weights was complaining about how much weight he had lost. "I gotta get some place where I can eat. I know I lost almost 20 lbs."

Later, he found out exactly how much he had lost. It was 22 lbs. to be exact. Our blood pressure, temperature, and weight were taken before we were loaded up again. The Atlanta facility was an outbreak waiting to happen. Men were coming in from various places, and it was no telling what they were exposed to as far as the flu, hepatitis, or TB. This is where you prayed hard and stayed away from having any unnecessary contact.

The shackles, chains, and cuffs went back on in the morning. The process felt no better and I had not gotten used to it and had no desire to make this a routine experience. For many, these procedures were now routine, because they were broken and no longer had the urge or will to fight or resist. They just went along with the program. I got a glimpse of a clock and saw that it was 4:30 a.m. I had lost all sense of time behind the fortified walls. There was no outside light to determine the time of day, weather, or anything of existence beside the cement walls and the iron that surrounded you. The air was stale and there were signs of rodents and roaches that figured they could also do a little time.

The sun was just coming up as we cleared the metal gates and barriers that were in place to fortify the sally port and loading areas. The drive to the airport was a makeshift convoy motorcade made up of three buses, a van, and three escort cars with heavily armed guards. At no point did we stop for lights. Atlanta traffic had not gotten backed up yet, so the ride to the airport was relatively short. I was thankful because another man was squeezed into the seat next to me. We both could not move and a ride longer than an hour would have us in bad shape. I already felt the circulation to my legs slowing down.

Once we arrived at the airport, we were driven onto a tarmac on the backside of the airport and lined up with two vans, two additional coach buses, and three mini-buses. There was clearly a system that would have overwhelmed the average person. However, it was routine for those running the transport. A generic white plane was less than 100 feet away. Everyone on my bus was unloaded and put in a single file line across the tarmac. Again, our names and numbers were checked.

Shockingly, for me, bodies began coming off the plane we were about to board. The women on board came out first. Some of them were in regular street clothes – probably the ones they were wearing when they were arrested. The others were in beige khaki prison attire. Every race and nationality was represented. As they walked down the stairs from the plane, I thought, "They better not misstep because the fall down that flight of stairs could be life ending. How would it be possible to break their fall with less than 2-inches of play in the shackled feet. They could not even use their hands to catch themselves. It would just be a hard landing."

As the men started coming down, an elderly man who had a cane and was not cuffed began making his way down the stairs. He was shackled, but looked much too weak to make it down the stairs. His legs shook, and trembled as he grabbed the rail with one arm, and leaned on his cane with the other. I was struggling with breaking out of the line to run and help him down the stairs. The guards that were close by looked away as if they had no interest at all. I heard other inmates whisper, "He ain't gonna make it." My heart raced and I could not even look in his direction anymore. Thirty seconds later I glanced in his direction to see that he had two steps left before he would be on the tarmac. In my mind, this was nothing short of a miracle.

Fifteen minutes later, it was my turn to climb onto *Con-Air*. I had traveled on literally hundreds of airplanes to numerous destinations, but none of my traveling experiences prepared me for this flight. The process was slow because there was a passage just inside the door where your handcuffs and shackles were rechecked. There were designated seats with plane monitors filling in for flight attendants. All the comforts of a plane had been stripped out and the seats were mismatched as if they were picked up at an old resale shop. The stale odor lingered from the last shipment of bodies and would have made the average person gag.

I was seated next to a young Hispanic man that looked to be about 30-years-old. He was sweating profusely. He then turned and asked me in broken English, "How do these things work?" At first, I thought he was talking about the seatbelts or something. Then I realized he meant the plane. This was the first time he had ever been on an airplane. It made me think about some of the men I had met at the prison camp. Some had never been out of their state until they were arrested. Now a man was getting on his first airplane ride, compliments of the U.S. Marshal and the Bureau of

Prisons. It was hard for me to process taking your first airplane ride as a convict in shackles.

Every seat was taken on what appeared to be an old DC-9, and it was filled to capacity. There were no safety briefings before takeoff, just a stern warning and hard looks that any incidents, challenges, or disruptions to the normal routine would not be tolerated.

Finally, we taxied to a runway and felt every bump, divot, and crack in the pavement along the way. With the engines fired up, we shook, rattled, and rolled down the runway. We were like the little engine that could. The engines moaned and groaned as it peaked to lift off. I was sitting directly behind the right wing on the window seat and it looked almost like the wing was flapping just to give a little extra boost. Once we were completely airborne, the ride smoothed out a bit. My first-time flyer looked as if he had just completed an intense work out. "Is it over? Is that it?"

I calmly nodded and said, "Yeah. For now." He did not look relieved.

I had this experience two more times until I ended up in Louisiana, about 15 minutes from Baton Rouge. I rode in a van about 45 minutes to a county jail. This place was like no other jail I had experienced working as an officer or an FBI agent. They worked off a different system and set of rules. Trustees ran the place with young deputy cadets assisting. They made up the rules along the way and did what they thought was appropriate at the time.

I was processed in with a photo, wristband, and the infamous brown paper bag meal. Without any dialogue, I was pushed into a holding cell, and then it was on. A drunk came in and he was ready to fight, cuss, and punish anyone he encountered during his stay. "What the hell are you looking at?"

The female processor fired back, "You ain't gonna talk to me that way. I will whip yo ass!" And she meant it. Even in his deep level of intoxication, the drunk recognized he did not want any of her. "Now stand up here and let me take your picture. Open up your eyes." It was clear that she was in control.

I thought to myself, "Kindness would win this lady over and maybe I could get a shower and some fresh clothes." But, before I could work my magic, she looked me in the eye and said, "I know who you are, they already called worrying me about what to do with you." I was somewhat relieved until the one-eyed trustee walked me to a heavy metal door with an eight by ten-inch window.

"You want something to read?" he asked in a raspy voice with his glass eye wondering.

Before I could answer him, he handed me a blanket and a small towel. Here is another suit in case you get cold. I was no longer wearing my paper-thin khakis I had been traveling in, but the shameful orange jump suit. I was not making a fashion statement, but the statement that I was a convict just like everyone else. I looked over at the books and asked, "Do you have a Bible?"

The trustee cocked his head towards me to look at me with his good eye. "Hold on, let me see. Go in there for a minute, and I will be right back."

I stepped into the cold cement cell, not realizing it would be my new home for the next forty-two days. The iron door slammed behind me. The bunk bed was smack dab in the center of the 10x15 space, with the stainless-steel toilet 12-inches from the head of the bed. There was a shower stall a foot from the toilet that was a simple indentation into the cinder block wall giving 2x2 feet of space to shower. It looked like it had not been used in months. A small steel table and metal stools were bolted to the floor across from the shower. The stench of recycled air filled what some would deem a luxury prison suite.

Ten minutes later, "Hit me on eight!" was yelled from a now familiar voice. The door buzzed and the lock popped. The trustee returned and he had a Bible in his hands. I was ready to go, and I picked up my blanket and orange jumpsuit. "Hold on. You got to wait here a minute until Mrs. Pam finishes." Before I could respond, he stepped on the other side of the door and slammed it shut.

"How long before she will be done?" was my immediate plea.

"I don't know, but I will send her over. While you wait, I'll get you something to eat." He was instantly gone out of sight from my small observation window.

There was no way of tracking time. I did not have a watch, and I could not see the clock from the angle I was looking in my cell. I was trying to estimate the time by the type of arrestees I could see being taken to the other cells. It looked like it might be around 9:00 p.m. or 10:00 p.m. I was leaning on the steel door, watching the way things ran in the jail. It felt like it had been at least an hour since I saw anyone go by and my mind started racing, trying to figure out a way to escape.

I started going over the process I went through coming in. I could tell the guards were very laid back and not well trained. I did not want to hurt anyone, but I needed to get their attention. I would have to take someone and threaten them to get the deputies in the control room to open the exit doors. I just did not know how far I would have to go. There were no guns or firearms allowed in the processing area, so I would have to use my hands. There were a lot of female deputies and they would be easy to take. The men were small and out of shape.

"Wait! What was I thinking....?" I was having thoughts that were not my own. I scared myself. "Was I losing my mind in this isolation?" I did not know and then I found myself sliding down the cold steel door beginning to weep and sob uncontrollably. There was no one to hear my cries and no one who cared. I lost track of how long I was in the puddle of tears, but when my eyes opened, they focused on the words HOLY BIBLE written in gold on the navy-blue canvas seam.

It was clearly a sign that I was not alone. I sifted through my pockets to find my glasses in my oversized orange jumpsuit. The simple and familiar words I turned to were:

"The Lord is my shepherd; I shall not want. He makes me to lie down in green pastures; He leads me beside the still waters. He restores my soul; He leads me in the paths of righteousness For His name's sake. Yea, though I walk through the valley of the shadow of death, I will fear no evil; For You are with me; Your rod and Your staff, they comfort me. You prepare a table before me in the presence of my enemies; You anoint my head with oil; My cup runs over. Surely goodness and mercy shall follow me All the days of my life; And I will dwell in the house of the Lord Forever." Psalms 23.

As soon as I read *forever*, my cell went black. The lights were out with nothing but light coming in through the window on the steel door to my cell.

The God That is With You in Every Storm

The two-inch metal flap fell open clanging against the door of my cell. The slot was filled with my usual meal tray. I got to my feet and squinted out my window trying to let my eyes adjust to the light. My stomach was growling, but what was supposed to be breakfast did not seem appetizing. I tasted the orange liquid in the Styrofoam cup and it was just colored, cold, sugar water. I drank it and gave the pleading look for seconds. After receiving seconds, I politely slid my tray back through the slot. "You ain't eating?" the trustee asked. He seemed insulted as if he had cooked the food himself.

This was my routine for the next 17 days. I drank as much as I could to keep from dehydrating, and then I was questioned by the doctor that was later determined to be unlicensed. Medical care was mandatory, but every jail and prison bid out to the cheapest provider. This was the second time I had been treated and examined by an unlicensed doctor.

I had fasted in the past, but this was a different type of fast. This fast was partially forced because of the horrible food. What a dichotomy, giving up food to survive. I remember reading when you do not eat, you become much more sensitive to your surroundings and what is going on spiritually. So, I noticed when

I read my Bible, I now understood the words from a different perspective than I had in the past.

My degree was in Theology, and I had read most passages in the Bible at least once. Now, many principles I had missed in the past were becoming real and practical. I began memorizing long passages in Proverbs that I recited out loud. When guards walked by, they would open my door, and check my cell to make sure no one else was in the cell. They would often question me briefly. I would always think to myself, "There were much more serious folks out in general population."

I recall one time when a fight had broken out and a couple of guys had beaten each other up pretty good. One was pulled into the processing area and, by the looks of it, had passed out. All I could see was a stretcher being brought in and other men yelling, "You should have killed his ass!" I began reading Mark 4:37,

> "And a great windstorm arose, and the waves beat into the boat, so that it was already filling. **38** But He was in the stern, asleep on a pillow. And they awoke Him and said to Him, "Teacher, do You not care that we are perishing?"**39** Then He arose and rebuked the wind, and said to the sea, "Peace, be still!" And the wind ceased and there was a great calm."

It had been missed in every storm I had ever faced, but now the words stood out like they were in neon lights, "Teacher, do

You not care that we are perishing?" I was asking the same question that Jesus' disciples were asking. I wanted to know if God cared. I was in the storm of my life, and I wanted to know if God cared. The reality was that I was not certain at all if God cared. I went back and read the passage several more times as if it was a riddle I was attempting to figure out. Each time I read it, another point jumped out. The first point that jumped out was the parallels between life and being out to sea.

During Jesus' time, if anyone was going to travel, trade, be productive, advance in any way, they would have to do so via the sea. Unfortunately, there were no weather reports to give predictions of high pressure, low pressure, wind directions, and Doppler reports. So, there was a high risk of going out to sea and facing storms that could arise out of nowhere. You took a risk. If the waters were rough, it would determine if the vessel you traveled in was sea worthy. You were literally taking your life into your own hands.

Over the centuries, stories were told about countless individuals who died in storms at sea. Even modern day tales have been told of tragic loss of life because of ice storms. For example, the Titanic, which was considered an unsinkable ship, sank on its maiden voyage.

In similar fashion, life can cause you to experience unexpected events you are in no way prepared for or equipped to handle. After about two weeks in the cell, this is exactly how I felt. I had gone through life believing Jesus was with me, but at this point in the worst storm of my life it felt like he was asleep and did not care.

Day after day, for six to eight hours at a time, I read the Bible and dissected the passages. I spent extended periods of time in Proverbs reading the chapter that was consistent with the date. I found myself almost memorizing the entire chapter. I would not put down my Bible until I had memorized a verse that meant the most to me in my present situation. For example, Proverbs 21:1, *"The king's heart is in the hand of the Lord, Like the rivers of water; He turns it wherever He wishes."*

After reading this passage, I was reminded of what I had read a year earlier and had expected God to do on my behalf. I believed God would change the heart of the judge, the prosecutor, someone with power that would come to my rescue and bring deliverance my way. It did not happen, but I still believed this verse was true. I wanted to shake Jesus, and wake him up and get him to change the heart of the king and speak peace to my storm. Again, it did not happen.

Two weeks later, I went to court and saw a defendant that was just starting the process of what I had gone through. I could not help him and did not have any idea of his fate. However, I wanted to ask him, "Was he equipped to survive his storm? What was motivating him to survive? Was anger, revenge, justice, or recognizing that he had a purpose to fulfill sustaining him in his storm, or did he realize that his storm was preparing him for something greater?" This was my new-found revelation driving and sustaining me. I believed God was preparing me for something greater.

I had already gone through anger, almost to the point of bitterness, and it was not the best motivator. It only left me looking for someone to blame, and lingering expectation that someone owed me something. Because, in my mind, I was a victim. The continued revelation for me was just as Jesus was in the boat with the disciples during their storm, He was also with me in my storm. He started revealing all the different ways that demonstrated He still cared.

Two weeks later, I was on my way back to Kentucky. The trip back seemed much more pleasant and I was more at peace. I still did not know all that I would experience or the people I would meet, but I was at peace. God had spoken peace to my raging storm.

I reclaimed my personal belongings which had been in storage for almost two and a half months. Walking back on the compound brought no anxiety because I was a veteran and had stories to tell. My first greetings were of shock and concern. It had slipped my memory that I had not shaved or cut my hair in over two months. There were no mirrors for me to see myself, so I had no idea that I looked like I had been in the wilderness eating wild locusts and honey. "Hey Mac! You ok? Where yah been? Man, what happened to you?"

"I'm good, man. Had to go to court."

"You want something to eat? You've lost a lot of weight." When I put my old clothes back on, I could see what they were talking about. The next question looming in everyone's mind was, did I go back to court to testify against someone? In other words, was I a *snitch*? I put that to rest right away because the *last* thing I wanted to be known as was a snitch.

The brothers from the church were glad to see me and gave me a warm welcome. Some seemed genuinely concerned about me. There were all kinds of stories that had circulated about what happened to me. The amazing thing about prison stories is when there is no information, guys get creative and make up stories. Guys will say anything that will get them an audience, and make them look like they have some special inside knowledge. The stories ranged from my being released early, to my being sick in the hospital on my death bed. The story that concerned me the most was that I may have had some affiliation with law enforcement. I appeared to be mildly concerned, so there would be no validation. When little attention was given, the next story was told. Within two days, I was accepted as the same old *Mac* who had come in six months earlier.

I was excited to go to the chapel service on my first Sunday back. There were new guys who I had not seen in service. I sat quietly, anticipating hearing testimonies and a great word from the chaplain. The truth is the chaplain was not considered a great preacher, but when you have not heard any preaching in two months, you settle for what you can get.

Within 10 minutes, I recognized the service was going in a different direction. The lights were turned off and the quick announcement was made. "Chap will not be here today. Instead, we will watch a DVD of church services." My heart sunk from disappointment. I had not been in a service in almost three months, and I had to come back and watch it on TV.

"Really?" I thought to myself. I felt anger, and my heart rate rising in me. I was ready to scream at God, "Why do you keep doing this to me?" Every time I have an expectation, and I am in need, I get nothing but disappointment. While I was having my mental tantrum with my head down, I heard a familiar sound. The music, the voices, the song...as I looked at the screen, I knew the people. A DVD of West Angeles Church was being played.

The week before I left to go on my incarcerated sabbatical, a box of DVD's and CD's had been sent in for the chapel. I had not gotten a chance to watch them, but I was familiar with the different messages that were sent. I instantly became homesick. My sickness was minimized when I focused on the familiar faces. Bishop Charles Blake approached the podium as I had watched him do live on many occasions from my balcony seat. Just the raspiness of his voice began soothing my soul. "Tell your neighbor, your hair is growing again."

I heard this sermon years earlier, but at this moment, it was as fresh as hot bread coming out of the oven. I sat up straight and listened on the edge of my seat. This message chronicled Samson's life highlighting his great strength and secret. He lost it when he laid his head in the wrong lap and told his secret. It reminded me and all the men in the chapel that sin will take you farther than you want to go, keep you longer than you want to stay, and cost you more than you want to pay.

Samson went through each one of these phases. He did not have any intention of telling Delilah the secret of his strength. As a matter of fact, he tricked her on several occasions. Regrettably, to his own demise, he continued to go back to Delilah. He ultimately gave in and told her the secret of his strength—sharing more than he intended.

He stayed too long, and received a haircut he did not request. There is something in all of us that will always try to test the limits and boundaries. Bishop Blake was masterful in illustrating this flaw in the life of Samson. We know there are consequences to every action, but for some reason, we believe we are exempt and end up staying where we should not, too long.

Very few of us count the cost of our actions beforehand. We may have an idea of what we believe it will cost, but find ourselves underestimating the expense. One of the men at the camp with me was a car salesman. He explained why he always wanted to run someone's credit. Once he got a person's credit score, he knew what they were worth and how much they would pay. It did not matter how much they intended to pay, the longer they stayed the more they paid.

Storms can have the same impact on us. They take us out further than we desire. The waves come and slow our progress, and keep us out in the deep much longer than we want. In the end, we can find ourselves shipwrecked, and paying more than we intended. I know this is the case in every storm that Jesus is not present.

When I look back at Luke 4:38, it makes it clear that Jesus was with them. Everyone is going to face a storm, but you do not want to face it alone. Even though Samson was in the storm and abandoned his personal code of ethics, disregarded God's instructions for his life, told the secret to his strength, lost his power, and became a defeated man; his life was not over. God was not finished with Samson. There are too many men who have told their secret, become defeated, and believed their life to be over. Even in Samson's defeat and failure, God was still with him. Bishop Blake proclaimed from his message, *Samson's hair began to grow*! The growth of Samson's hair proclaimed that he was not going to remain in a defeated state. Judges 16:21-22 (NKJV),

> *"21 Then the Philistines took him and put out his eyes, and brought him down to Gaza. They bound him with bronze fetters, and he became a grinder in the prison. 22 However, the hair of his head began to grow again after it had been shaven."*

158 / THE GOD THAT IS WITH YOU IN EVERY STORM

God was still with him in his storm. I looked around the room as the men's eyes were glued to the screen. I saw heads nodding, I heard whispers of, "Amen." I looked to the other side of the room and saw tears flowing down hard cheeks from eyes that stated, "Real men don't cry in prison." Men that had stopped hoping, believing, and trying, now believed their hair would grow again. These men were now captivated by the power of God's word.

This was the exact message I needed to hear. I was ready to stand to my feet and praise God as if I were in the West Angeles Cathedral in Los Angeles. I felt the power of God as Bishop Blake concluded his message. In the natural sense, I had just shaved my head bald to improve my abandoned appearance from my extended road trip. In an emotional and spiritual sense, I felt my hair growing back. It was amazing to see how God had me return for this exact Sunday to hear this exact message. I thought to myself, "He is with me. He does care about me."

But, as I was thinking the message was just for me, after the chapel service, men began walking up to me, "Hey man that message was for me."

"That preacher was talking to me."

"Man, my hair is starting to grow." It never ceases to amaze me how a real word from God speaks to everyone in room. It softens even the hardest hearts to let them know He is with them in their storm and He cares. The storm Samson experienced, he had brought upon himself—just as many of the men had brought their storms upon themselves. They had gone further than they wanted to go, stayed longer than they wanted to stay, and paid more than they wanted to pay, but God would still allow their hair to grow back.

While walking back to my room, the inmate chaplain, *TJ*, welcomed me back and told me he had a project for me. Without inquiring too much, I accepted. So, he told me we would talk the next day. When I returned to my cube, I climbed up into my bunk for the afternoon still thinking about the sermon. One of the reasons God allows your hair to grow back is He still wants to use you. He has plans for your life. I was about to quickly discover that He was going to use me in this prison much sooner than I expected.

The next day, I was reintroduced to a Chinese young man, *Andy*. With all sincerity, TJ explained, "Andy wants to know more about Jesus and have someone to teach him how to study the Bible. I want you to mentor him." I was in shock and responded accordingly.

"Hey, TJ! I'm not sure if this is really going to be a good fit." Andy spoke broken English and was kind of known as a hustler. The truth was, I had not taken the time to get to know him. "Well, look man, I'll try to help him, but I can't be chasing him down." We walked towards Andy's cube where he was running his store. I just started shaking my head, saying to myself, "This guy is a true hustler."

In broken English, "Hey, my man! What's up? You gonna teach me Bible? Heard you the best." Before I could proclaim I had nothing in common with Andy, and I did not think it was going to work, we were set to meet the next day.

Andy showed up at my cube 10 minutes early. "Mac, what you doin? Chillin?" Before I could get offended by Andy trying to sound black, I had to realize he was just trying to blend and fit in a place where he was the true minority. Out of 500 inmates, there were only six Asians and, under normal circumstances, they would not even speak to each other.

There were two Koreans, two Chinese, a Vietnamese, and one who said he was mixed, but leaned more towards Japanese because that was his native language. I had learned from my cultural diversity training with the Bureau that the different ethnicities did not want to be mixed together, nor did they care for one another. But in prison, being the minority caused them to bond.

Andy was a little different. He was a natural born leader, and you could tell right away he was, what we label, a strong type A personality. He was naturally smart and caught onto the things that people liked to gain their trust. Initially, I was cautious, but he broke me down because he came bearing gifts; his famous egg rolls that he hand made and fried in the kitchen. I had heard about these egg rolls, but never tasted one myself. They smelled delicious. "Here Mac. I brought you something because I heard you lost weight."

I laughed, "Is it that obvious."

"Get your weight up Mac, in case you have to handle your business." It made no difference if you were in the church or not, you always had to be ready to fight. Fighting was not encouraged, but you had to be ready. *Keeping your weight up* was an expression used to stay in shape by lifting weights, so you did not appear weak.

"Go ahead. Have one. They are for you. No charge," Andy said with a big smile. I took one out of the plastic bag and felt that it was still warm. I bowed my head slightly to pray over it and took a bite. To this day, it is by far the best egg roll I have ever had in or out of prison. I heard Andy had his own restaurant on the street, but Andy was the real deal. Not a pretend wanna be cook. He took pride in his food from the preparation to the presentation.

All my anxiety was gone after I finished eating. "Ok, are you serious about learning the Bible? Why?" Andy began to share his story. He grew up literally dirt poor in the countryside of South China. To him, *dirt* was synonymous with being *poor*. His parents could not afford a baby sitter, so they would leave Andy and his brother alone in their dirt floor hut with a bowl of rice to eat for at least eight hours a day. They would spend the entire day playing in the dirt. When he was 11-years-old, he migrated to the United States and learned English as best he could. He started working for an uncle at age 12 and stopped going to school regularly. He opened his own restaurant at age 19 and took off from there. The family religion was Buddhist, but now he wanted to know more about Jesus since he had accepted Christ as his Lord and Savior.

We set a time to meet twice a week for about an hour. I had no idea how serious Andy was about studying the Bible. The more I gave him, the more he wanted. He would read a chapter and come back with plenty of questions. He started memorizing scriptures to the point that he could quote them in English and Chinese. He had a dual-language parallel Bible that had the scriptures in English and Chinese.

Then he hit me with a request that seemed to come out of nowhere. "Mac, I want to learn how to pray. I don't know how to pray." It was a sincere request I could not take lightly.

"Well, I can help you learn how to pray." The truth was, no one had ever asked me to teach them how to pray, and I was not sure where to start. Then I asked, "What do you want to tell God?"

"I don't know. I want to pray like you and the other brothers."

Then, it hit me. Andy had never prayed in public before and was not sure if he could do it like everyone else. I then explained to him that he was not praying for everyone else, but he was praying to God. God was not so concerned about the words he was speaking as much as how was the heart that it was coming from.

To help Andy learn how to pray, we started with a form I had learned early in my life that had become natural for me. It was the A.C.T.S. prayer method. I tried to simplify it as much as possible. "A" stands for acknowledge God for who He is and how great He is. C stands for confess. Confess your sins and your need for God in your life. T represent thanks. Express your thankfulness to God. Thank Him for everything good and bad. Last, but not least, the S is for supplications."

"What's that, Mac?" Andy looked at me strange because he had no clue what that meant. He had been writing vigorously taking notes. I quickly simplified it.

"That just means you can ask God for something. Ask for others first, then for yourself." Andy nodded his head that he understood and had an excitement and enthusiasm that attracted others.

When Andy *left* my cube, I was going to lay down and read, which usually turned into a nap. I could not start because another young man was outside my cube asking if he could talk to me. I knew him, and we shared the commonality of being from Chicago. He was straight to the point with his request. "I don't know my purpose Bro. Mac, and I need someone to help me." I did not know how to respond at first. Here was this 6' 4", 250 lbs. former gang member that was all tatted up, wiping a tear away, asking me to help him.

"I heard you were mentoring Andy and helping him. Can you squeeze me in with a little time?" There was no hesitation, I would not have to squeeze him in, or make something happen. I recognized this young man and four others were part of my purpose. *My hair was starting to grow.*

Freedom

While completing my 36 months, I purposed in my heart not to come home an angry and bitter man who had been let down by our justice system. The desires and feelings of rage, mistrust, and frustration were there, but I could not give in to them and allow them to consume me. I constantly prayed, "God, if you allowed this storm to take place in my life, it has to have a purpose. Father, let some good come out of this." This experience was bigger than me, so I believed it was making me and those I was connected to better, including my cellmate.

Jack was a no-nonsense guy who made it clear he did not have time for *foolishness*. "My name is Jack. I can share this room with you, but I cannot put up with a lot of foolishness."

I laughed in my response, "That makes two of us."

We were about the same age, but he was from the South. The next thing he said was, "I need someone that will pray with me." I then began to listen to Jack's story. Jack never explained to me why he was in prison, but he did let me know his wife had cancer. Prior to coming to prison, he took her for treatments once a month. With him now being in prison, he was concerned about how she would get to her treatments. I watched this man's countenance change after we finished speaking. I could see the guilt, remorse, and frustration consuming him with every word he spoke. "Man, I hope she holds on for these next 18 months until I get out of here."

After hearing Jack's story, I could no longer focus on my own problems. I wanted to help my cellmate through his storm that began to intensify after he spoke with his daughter. The thing Jack feared most was happening; his wife was in the hospital. There was no doubt Jack loved his family. He had taken up half of the wall with family photos, cards, and he beamed with pride when he spoke about his young grandson.

"Mac, it doesn't look good," as a lone tear began to roll down his hard-chiseled cheek. Jack's greatest fear was never seeing his wife alive again, and rightfully so. There were numerous painful stories of how men were not allowed to visit sick family members in the hospital or attend the funerals of those who died. Sadly, there was no closure for these men. Consequently, no one wanted to get a call to report to the chaplain's office to visit the, *Grim Reaper*.

In a hushed whisper, "I need to be at home making sure she gets the right treatment." He shook his head as if he was attempting to tell death, "no." Personally, I hated dealing with death and people who were sick because I felt my words were always so inadequate. I realized through this experience that it was not about what I said, but about being there to listen. I listened in the middle of the day, at breakfast, on long walks, and just about any time he needed to talk. There were questions about

God, justice, and sickness, of which the answer was always prayer.

As I returned from one of my monthly visits with my family; I was riding high and feeling good. When I turned to walk into my cell, there was Jack on his knees praying. He was in the center on my bunk. So, my plans to lay down and day dream about my visit were quickly canceled. All kinds of thoughts went through my mind, "Had his wife gotten worse? Had she died? Was he losing it? Maybe he just needed to pray." I went to the bathroom and returned only to find him still there. I did not want to disturb him, so I opted for the TV room. The room was packed with the normal football heads seeing if they won their bets for the day.

After 20 minutes, I returned to the room to find it empty. It was as if all was normal because the room was the way I left it before my visit. I looked out the window and saw Jack out on the *weight pile*. The weight pile was old, real, steel weights that had become an escape for men to work out more than just their bodies. They worked out their frustrations, pain, and disappointment. You saw men driving their bodies with a motivation that was much deeper and bigger than themselves. Something was going on with Jack, and it showed on the weight pile. Less than an hour ago he was praying, and now he was lifting everything he could.

He finally walked in when it was time for count. I could see it in his eyes when he entered the cell. I did not have to ask what was going on. "Mac, I don't know what God is doing, but

He promised to keep her alive until I get home. I have three months left and I hope she makes it."

In the following three months, I watched Jack transfer his own pain to help others. He helped get men together every night at 9:30 p.m. to pray in the laundry room. He listened to the requests of the men and asked me to pray. He fought against having pity parties because he recognized his purpose in prison was greater than his pain. Still, those three months were not without challenges.

It was a dark day when one of our prison brothers, who asked us to pray for his seven-year-old daughter, received word she had lost her fight against cancer. I could not imagine losing my child, especially while in prison. Even though he was without his daughter, he was not without support. Fifty of us came together to encourage and pray for our brother. Our prayer was not just that God would comfort him, but he also needed a miracle. The funeral was 300 miles away in Alabama, and he needed $500. We prayed and coupled our prayers with action. Within two hours, the money was raised and he was leaving the next day.

Even though this seemed to have a semi-happy ending because the brother could go to his daughter's funeral, Jack was devastated by our brother's loss. This was too close to home for Jack. The next morning Jack had a tremendous amount of anxiety. "Mac, we have to talk." Again, I listened more than I spoke. He was short and on edge. I stepped in when one of the guys tried to push his buttons not knowing what was behind Jack's edginess.

"Jack, you are on a mission. You are trying to get home to your family? This guy has no one to go home to." Jack nodded his head that he understood, but not without making his statement.

"Mac, I don't have time for foolishness." Ultimately, Jack stayed focused. I was proud of him and thankful to God that three months later, he went home. Thankfully, his wife was alive and still in the fight. After a while, I was happy to finally hear from Jack. He wrote me, and I spoke with him on the phone to hear about how she was getting better. In another three months, it would be time for me to go home. I was thankful I was not going home to a sick wife, sick children, or sick brothers and sisters.

The last 90 days I focused on myself physically, mentally, and spiritual. I lost 20 lbs., studied the Bible and prayed with a greater concentration. I wanted to be in the best shape in every area of my life, physically, mentally, and spiritually. In my heart, I knew I could not go home bitter. If I did, it would be like going home with the flu. I would spread my bitterness and my entire family would be infected. In turn, they would continue to spread the bitterness to anyone they encountered. I had to go home better, not bitter.

No one knew when I was leaving, but when I got my date, I wrote notes to ten brothers. I wanted to encourage them and express my appreciation for the blessing they had been to me during my time in prison. When my day came, I chose to leave without any fanfare. I came quietly into prison, and I wanted to leave even quieter. At 12:15 a.m., a flashlight was shined in my room. "McAllister!"

"Yes!"

"Time to go." I followed the guard through the pitch-black dorm. Everyone was in bed, asleep, or reading. I carried my bag, so few could see it. The cool fall air was crisp, so I had on my sweats to stay warm. I never looked back, as I followed the guard the 100 yards to the Administration Building. My storm was coming to an end. I was free.

No Place Like Home

I would soon realize my freedom was not the freedom I left behind 36 months ago. I had no job and no offers waiting. I was going to a halfway house that was overcrowded and run by an organization whose goal was getting paid. This is when I found out just how much the housing part of the criminal justice system is a money-making business. During my intake, my past attachment to law enforcement was quietly acknowledged by the intake worker at the half way house.

The goal was for me to obtain a job and get home as quickly as possible. When I was not looking for a job, I taught a career and interviewing class to over 25 men to help them obtain employment when they were released. I found that some of the men had never had a legitimate job. All the concepts were abstract for almost half of the men. Now I had to practice what I *preached*.

My first interview was canceled because the manager was not available. I was immediately filled with anxiety. I thought to myself, "Did she know I was a convicted felon and refuse to meet with me?" I doubted myself and was immediately discouraged. I was told to come back tomorrow. Initially, I did not have a ride, but before the day was out, I had two offers to take me to my interview.

On my second interview attempt, I was told that the manager was still not available, but the assistant manager offered to interview me and pass my application to the manager. Within the first minute, I got the elephant out of the room and informed her that I had been convicted of a felony. I explained the circumstances and my past employment history. I noticed that she looked away as her eyes began to fill with water and tears fall.

"Wow! That could have been me," were her next words. "I lost everything after a loan officer falsified one of my loan applications. I was investigated by the FBI and everything. It was identical to what you just told me, except I was a real estate agent." I listened and nodded my head. She wiped her tears and told me that I had her vote and she would recommend me to the manager. Then, in a hushed tone, "You don't have any drug problems, do you?" But, before I could answer no, she said, "Good!" She handed me a form. "Take this right down the street. There is a lab there that does our drug testing. You can start as soon as your results come back." She stood up, shook my hand and walked me to the door.

An overwhelming feeling of confidence came over me, because someone wanted to give me a chance, and I could work some place besides a prison. Still, I wanted a back-up plan just in case someone changed their mind; or the manager did not want to take a chance, so I applied and got two more jobs, both in the restaurant industry. I was working 16 hours a day and six days a week.

Two weeks later, my goal was realized. I was going home. My home had not changed much physically, but the family had changed dramatically. My young girls were now young ladies, who no longer laughed at my silly jokes, but they were now respectful and cordial. The greatest absence was my son. He took on the temporary role of *the man of the house,* but he was now away in the Air Force. There was no more father and son time. However, the real challenge was reconnecting with my best friend of almost 30 years, my wife. We had talked, written, and visited during my three years' absence, but now I was home. She had changed and I had changed, but not together. We changed independently and there were noticeable differences. My wife, Judy, has always been independent, taking the initiative to get things done. Somehow, I had to work my way back into her life.

I was now in the aftermath of my storm and facing the *collateral damage.* I survived the storm only to see the impact it had on my home, my relationships, and my level of confidence. I found myself being isolated to one room in the house. Not that I was restricted, but complacent to one dimension. To compensate for my clear dysfunction at home, I stayed away, working my three jobs to minimize my time at home. I did not want to work through what I had lost. I did not want to sift through the rubble and rebuild. Thankfully, I stumbled upon an article about New Orleans five years after Hurricane Katrina. While reading the article, I started making comparisons and identifying with the similarities of my personal storm.

The article highlighted who stayed, who left, and who came back to New Orleans. The article about those who came back, got my attention. Even though they came back to a different city, they came back because of love. There were characteristics they loved about New Orleans. That love was now the motivation behind the rebuilding process. In the end, they simply wanted to recapture the specific uniqueness of the city they still loved.

The article shook me from my denial. I had to rebuild my relationships at home. I loved my family deeply, and with the help of God, I was going to start rebuilding. I quit two of my jobs, so I could spend more time with my family. I worked 40 hours a week, went to school functions, church, movies, the gym, and anything else I could do to rebuild and re-establish my relationship individually and collectively with my family. Also, it was important for me to express, to them, the pride I felt for how they carried themselves throughout our storm. Part of the rebuilding required my taking responsibility for their pain. So, I apologized and told them how sorry I was for what my absence had caused them to experience.

When I left, my youngest daughter was 10 years old and in the 5th grade. Now she was a *big* 8th grader, straight "A" student, ready for the world. Even though she has always been extremely bright and mature for her age, we thought it was best to protect her from the stories surrounding my trial and imprisonment. In many ways, she went through her own personal storm.

"Baby girl, how have you been handling things with me being gone?"

"Ok...Will you be able to come to my basketball game?"

"Sure! I'm home now, and I won't miss any of your games. I will be right there." Those few words put a huge smile on her face. "I'm sorry for all of the other games I missed. I can't wait to see you play. I heard you were playing on the varsity team in 6th grade."

"Yeah, I'm doing the best I can."

My older daughter was much more withdrawn. At 16, she had few words for me. She wanted to get her permit and have the freedom and independence to drive. I recognized that it was important to her, so I took the opportunity to reestablish our relationship. While we rode around, we talked about how she felt about what happened. "I really missed you, but I knew there was nothing I could do about it." I made another feeble attempt to apologize, but that is not what she wanted. She desired to move forward, and put the past behind us.

It was not until almost two years later, on her 18th birthday that I realized how she felt. On her birthday, I asked her, "What have you learned in these 18 years?"

"I've learned how to forgive, and put the past behind me and move towards the future." With those words, I knew I had been forgiven, and no longer needed to wrestle with the guilt that had been plaguing me since my return.

When Judy and I attempted to process through our feelings, her words were always direct, "I'm full. I don't even know where to start because there is so much. There is so much I want to say, and I need to say. I feel if I start, I might not ever stop; I might say something hurtful." I did not believe Judy's intent was to hurt me, but it was clear she was deeply wounded. She questioned our future, and how we would spend it.

"What can I do to make things better, and help us get back to normal?"

"What's normal to you is no longer normal for me. I've changed. We have all changed."

I started to question if that meant her love had changed. In one of our many heart-to-heart conversations, Judy expressed something that was extremely profound, "I didn't want to look back at this period of my life and be ashamed and embarrassed at how I handled it." I was speechless. Her words were more than thought provoking. They went straight to the heart of who we are and why we do what we do. She had every right to be bitter, but she wasn't. She had been thrown into being a single parent without cause. She had done nothing to be left with the sole responsibility of three children. There was no more *me time* for her. There was no down time, no breaks, and she would not give any excuse for making sure everything was in order.

I had to finally come to the realization, it was going to take time to rebuild. If rebuilding our family was going to happen, remaining consistent with my words, actions, and commitment were necessary materials to cause our family to survive. But, forgiveness and love would be the glue to hold us all together.

At some point, survivors must take the time to rebuild what was lost. You may have to build with different materials, but if the foundation is love; you will build again. In some way or another, we are all survivors. Have you ever asked yourself, "Why did *I* survive? Was my survival by luck, by chance, or was it just not my time?" I have come to the realization that your survival, my survival, our survival, was a divine appointment for a divine assignment. No true purpose in life is absent of the storms of adversity. Some storms give warning signals while others completely blindside us. Regardless of how the storm hits, what will you do now that you have survived? I take inspiration from a living basketball legend, Earvin "Magic" Johnson. Jr.

I was in church the Sunday Magic accepted Jesus Christ as his personal Savior. The world did not know what he was going to announce in the days that followed, but he boldly confronted his storm head on. Instead of hiding, he accepted that his life was changed forever. Magic came to terms that his storm did not come to end his life, but to empower him to help others. He became an advocate for those diagnosed with HIV/AIDS. He grew in his faith and trust in God to help him push past his pain into his purpose. He boldly acknowledges he would not have accomplished anything without God.

From one survivor to another, *"Don't give in. Don't give out. and Don't give up."* These words are not just catch phrases, but foundational principles that helped me to push past my pain to my purpose.

You can't *give in* to the temptation to quit. Often, the pain becomes so great, it leads to overwhelming frustration. In those moments, you may be tempted to do things outside of your character or walk away from your commitments. But, you *can't give in.*

You *can't give out.* There is an unconditional love that only comes from God when you recognize what He gave first. He gave his son, Jesus Christ, so you would not run out of the faith to believe and trust Him with your life. Even when it seems like he is asleep on the boat, he still cares and will speak peace during the storm. You *can't give out.*

You *can't give up* on believing you can be restored to good health, live a happy life, and fulfill God's purpose for your life. Giving up means you are no longer resisting the temptations to live a life outside of your purpose. So, many have given up by choice, and others seemingly were forced. I love the song, "Don't give up on God, because He won't give up on you. He's able!" We *can't give up* because, "…God is more than able to do exceedingly abundantly above all that we ask or think…" (Ephesians 3:20) I love the verse, "...Eye has not seen, nor ear heard, neither have entered into the heart of man, the things which God has prepared for them that love him." (1 Corinthians 2:9)

I get it. Storms can cause your love for God to disappear because you feel abandoned and alone in the storm. You cannot just go by what you feel. In a storm, you can rely on what you know. You only know God by spending time with Him. Just like I had to quit my extra jobs and spend time with my family, you can cut some things out of your life to spend time with God in prayer and reading His word.

I am back in Los Angeles now, and I frequently travel through Beverly Hills and see unbelievable signs of wealth and success. I used to be in awe and aspire to have the same. However, my storm changed my perspective. Now, I frequently serve and go down to *Skid Row* and The Mission. I see people that barely made it through their storm. However, because of what I have been through, I connect and identify with them not out of pity, but from a place of empathy. I want them to know that the same God who brought me through my storm will bring them through.

You may be in a storm, coming out of a storm, or about to go through a storm; no matter where you are, make sure God is with you. The stories that you have read are more than just stories. They are real-life experiences that were unexpected. We could have easily allowed ourselves, our dreams, and our hopes to die. We are yet rebuilding, restructuring, and repositioning ourselves for God's greater purpose. The losses were great, and in many ways, unimaginable. Even so, it always amazes me how what is lost is always replaced with something better when God is with you. It is not understandable at the time, but God really does make, *"all things work together for good that love Him and are called according to His Purpose."* (Romans 8:28)

Finally, if you have been blessed, inspired, and encouraged by this book, please share it. But, more than that, take the time to share your time, talents, and treasure with those who are in a storm. By making this type of investment, you create more survivors. As well, you can be the lifeboat of comfort, the lighthouse of guidance, and the lifeline of hope. Let others know they are not alone, and that God gives us His grace to make it through to be a Survivor of Storms.

If you are a survivor, please declare this with me:

I survived my storm for a purpose. My purpose is greater than the pain I endured. My purpose is to bring hope, healing, and a heavenly perspective to Earth. I will spread the love of God everywhere I go, and be a light in the midst of darkness. It is through light that survivors are found after the storm. I can rest assure that storms will come, so I am ready to let my light shine, through my talents, treasure, and time.

Made in the USA
San Bernardino, CA
05 July 2017